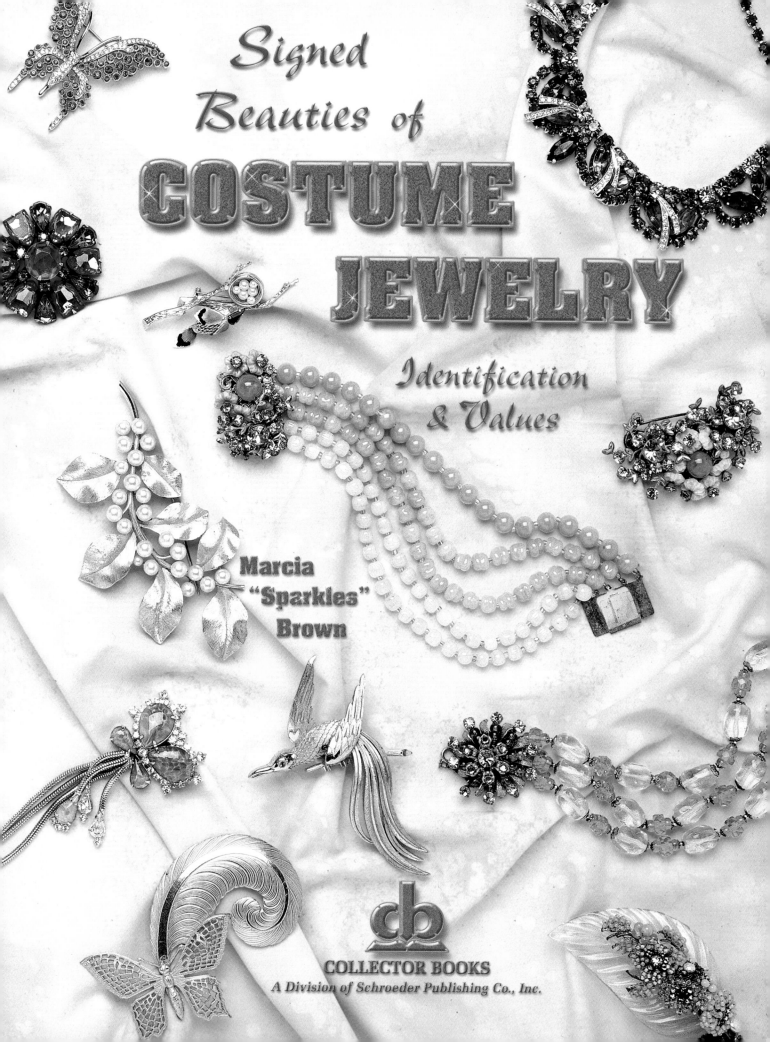

Signed Beauties of COSTUME JEWELRY

Identification & Values

Marcia "Sparkles" Brown

COLLECTOR BOOKS

A Division of Schroeder Publishing Co., Inc.

Also by this Author:
Unsigned Beauties of Costume Jewelry, Collector Books, 2000

Cover design by Terri Hunter
Book design by Joyce Cherry

COLLECTOR BOOKS
P.O. Box 3009
Paducah, Kentucky 42002-3009
www.collectorbooks.com

Copyright © 2002 Marcia Brown

All rights reserved. No part of this book may be reproduced, stored in any retrieval system, or transmitted in any form, or by any means including but not limited to electronic, mechanical, photocopy, recording, or otherwise, without the written consent of the author and publisher.

The current values in this book should be used only as a guide. They are not intended to set prices, which vary from one section of the country to another. Auction prices as well as dealer prices vary greatly and are affected by condition as well as demand. Neither the author nor the publisher assumes responsibility for any losses that might be incurred as a result of consulting this guide.

Searching For A Publisher?

We are always looking for people knowledgeable within their fields. If you feel that there is a real need for a book on your collectible subject and have a large comprehensive collection, contact Collector Books.

Contents

This is the guardian of my hidden treasures.
Griffin: a classical, mythological, fabulous animal having a lion's body and legs, an eagle's head and wings, and a serpent's tail. The creature, symbolizing the union of strength and vigilance, lived especially in Asiatic Scythia where it guarded gold and gems and punished human greed by killing travelers who sought to take such treasure.

—*Encyclopedia Americana*

Acknowledgments

Everyone has been so supportive and kind to me. Collecting and sharing my passion for rhinestones has given me more rewards than I had ever thought possible. My husband, Kenneth A. Brown, is now my jewelry repair person and my photographer. We have developed a policy that clearly states that when he is performing these duties, I am in charge, and with that understanding we have found a mutual enjoyment and appreciation for the craftsmen and artisans of the jewelry industry.

Through my friends, Adelle Blevins, Julia McKinney, and Lois Mortensen I have had the opportunity not only to enlarge my own collection but also to expand my personal knowledge.

Having received so much, I am delighted to present to you what I now call my Beautiful Books. As a collector foremost, the more I learn about the American art form, Rhinestone Jewelry, the more I have become fascinated with the wonderful history and jewelry designs of manufacturers and designers that we, as collectors, have come to love.

In this my second Beautiful Book, I have selected designers that will fascinate and enthrall you. There are so many companies to choose from, and it was very difficult for me to select the ones I wanted to cover in this volume. Those you will meet will expose you to this wonderful sparkling world of delight. With diligent shopping in antique shows and stores and with extra luck, you may still uncover that rare hidden treasure at any garage or tag sale.

Marcia Brown published her first book, *Unsigned Beauties of Costume Jewelry* in 2000. She is the host and co-writer of the award-winning Venture Entertainment books-on-tape series *Hidden Treasures: A Collector's Guide to Antique & Vintage Jewelry*. Awards won in 1998 include the AEGIS, the Communicator, JOEY Award of Excellence, and the CINDY. Drawing upon 12 years of experience as a free-lance newspaper correspondent, she is a frequent contributor to *The Daze* (Otisville, MI), the Vintage Fashion & Costume Jewelry (Glen Oaks, NY), and various antique publications.

As an antique and vintage jewelry historian, lecturer, and collector, she has shared her knowledge and jewelry with such organizations as the American Association University Women, Republican Women, Regional Medical Assante Auxiliary, Christian Women, Rogue Valley Medical, and Providence Adult Care. She has also provided off-campus seminars for Oregon State University and private consultations for many dealers, mall owners, and collectors.

Since September 1996 she has served as the rhinestone jewelry advisor and contributor for *Schroeder's Antiques Price Guide* and *Garage Sale & Flea Market Annual*.

She is often seen at West Coast antique shows at the Robby/Don Miller identification and evaluation booth where patrons seek her expert opinion and advice about their jewelry.

An active member of Southern Oregon Antiques & Collectibles Club, she has served on its board for five years. For the past two years, Ms. Brown has chaired the Community Collect Display for the Southern Oregon Historical Society. She currently resides in the beautiful Oregon Rogue River Valley.

Introduction

In my first book *Unsigned Beauties of Costume Jewelry*, we learned about the basics of costume jewelry: the different cuts and shapes involved in designing beautiful, sparkling pieces; the different types of plating that gave the finishing touch. Establishing the decade when the piece was manufactured was also clearly outlined. Most important of all, identifying quality was stressed. All of the aspects were discussed to help develop your discerning eye and taste buds.

Now that you have graduated at the top of your class, let's go to the next level of collecting — signed jewelry. This is the stage where you should be fairly versatile with a magnifying glass or loupe. Your first step will be to turn the jewelry piece over to examine the back. This is a good practice whether the piece is signed or not because you can spot repairs or broken solders, missing parts of the pin back or missing parts of the piece (e.g., a butterfly's antennae).

Now, take that loupe and carefully go over the back inch by inch. Many times the company logo was on the master mold and after a peice was finished, the piece was plated, thus partially obscuring the logo.

Look on the necklace hook, the bracelet clasp, the side of the brooch pin, and the backs of the earrings.One of my favorite tales is of a beautiful parure of cocoa brown and apricot crystal beads that were for sale at an antique show. The dealer informed me that they were unsigned, despite my acclaiming that they surely must be signed. After much discussion on their beauty, I went home with the beautiful bracelet, necklace, and earrings.

In the strong sunlight at my work bench, I took out my loop and carefully searched for a signature. Nothing on the necklace, on the bracelet, nor the first earring I examined. Then, eureka, there was the name on the last earring. Re-evaluating my purchase, I realized it was worth three times what I paid for it.

When you find that anticipated signature, you can immediately raise the value of the jewelry at least 10% and as much as 30% if it is a hard-to-find company.

Come along with me now, and I'll introduce you to some companies, complete with pictures, so you can learn their styles and ways to spot the ones you would like within any display at an antique show.

Midwestern Connection

The Midwest had a very active clothing industry, centered in Chicago, Illinois back in the 1930s. The Great Lakes provided the shipping lanes, and the railroads were also well traveled for this great city. The rails were bringing in cattle for the meat industry, and business were on the upswing. There were money and millionaires, all the elements to create a market for the finer things in life. Shoppers wanted the latest fashions and the finest jewelry.

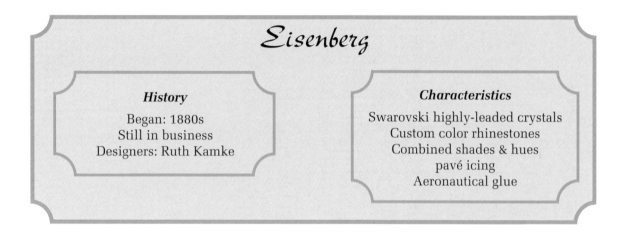

Eisenberg

History

Began: 1880s
Still in business
Designers: Ruth Kamke

Characteristics

Swarovski highly-leaded crystals
Custom color rhinestones
Combined shades & hues
pavé icing
Aeronautical glue

Jonas Eisenberg immigrated from Austria in the late 1800s. The young man settled in Chicago and found the thriving Midwestern city provided a wonderful beginning for his ambitions.

His women's wear firm opened in 1880. Sales franchises were sold to only the major department stores. In the beginning there were 500 franchises in the United States, and a decision was wisely made to limit the franchises to one per city to retain the exclusiveness. Thus each store would have the privilege of selling the fashion line that would draw women from miles around to that particular store.

A sharp business eye combined with memories of the glass works of his native birthplace, Tyrol, Austria, ignited a spark that became a bewitching flame to women. That region produced highly leaded Austrian crystals that gave brilliance to jewelry and were exported to the United States by the Austrian Swarovski firm in a quantity to meet Eisenberg's requirements.

Eisenberg made his ready-to-wear women's fashions unique with the gorgeous brilliance of a rhinestone brooch. Jewelry work was contracted out to such wholesale firms as Chicago-based ORA which quickly began designing and manufacturing the unmarked brooches to compliment the costumes.

Eisenberg Originals fashions made their mark, but soon franchises were reporting that the glittering jewels were being taken off the dresses and disappearing from the store.

Jonas's sons, Samuel and Harold, had taken over their father's clothing business in 1914. The two brothers found the rhinestone brooches were more popular than the dresses. Due to the Depression, women who were unable to buy new wardrobes were dressing up last year's dresses with jewelry from Eisenberg Originals. The clarity and sparkling of those Austrian stones set in sterling warmed up the "left-over fashions." Previously manufactured brooches had been unmarked, but now Eisenberg Originals proudly identified to all the jewelry's origins.

In 1935, Fallon and Kappel of New York were commissioned to create Eisenberg accessories, and the brothers decided in 1937 to separate the clothing and jewelry lines.

Ruth M. Kamke was one of their chief jewelry designers from 1940 to 1972. Her artistic use of sparkling rhinestones in settings that enhanced their icy whiteness drew comments that the jewelry pieces sparkled like winter's ice. Eisenberg Ice, so it was called, and so it was named, beginning the classic line of jewelry that continues today.

In 1940 when $30.00 to $40.00 was a woman's average weekly salary, Eisenberg sold their popular creations for $50.00 to $100.00. And the working girl was willing to spend three weeks salary for an Eisenberg. Of course, it was then bought on the layaway program, but the piece would soon be hers to wear.

Rhodium was used exclusively during the 1940s and 1950s because of its durability and non-tarnishing qualities. Smaller, brighter rhinestones were used to create the Snowflake brooches that incorporated dramatic shades of the same color to emphasize the jewelry design. Dramatic shadings from pink to red, pink to lavender take your breath away. The monochromatic shadings give a saturation of color to each brooch.

From 1950 to 1975, Eisenberg omitted marking their jewelry which has greatly disappointed many a collector. If a piece is unmarked, despite all of its fine workmanship and any claims, it cannot be identified or evaluated as an Eisenberg. The exception would be a piece of paper which would authenticate the purchase, or the presence of the original box.

The firm that had started out selling women's ready-to-wear silenced their sewing machines forever in 1958 to concentrate on the company's profitable costume jewelry line.

In 1969 a third generation took over the reins of command when grandson Karl Eisenberg became president. His influence can be found in the 1970s enamel jewelry, using the artistic designs of impressionist painters Picasso, Calder, Braque, Chagall, and Miro. Once ignored by collectors, this enamel jewelry is going up in value and is again being collected.

All rhinestones had been hand-set up to 1975 when they went to prong set, and/or glue. The glue was a space-age adhesive that had been formerly used to adhere a propeller to an engine.

This Chicago company continues to carry on the fine Eisenberg tradition. Karl Eisenberg is president of the company, now called Eisenberg Classics.

Top: Décolleté brooch made of twin diamente dress clips, hinged at the middle petal of the bottom flower to form a V. $525.00. Middle: 1930s dress accessory has a button shank to allow it to be sewn on. Red cabochon flower petals surround a green rhinestone center to create a floral bouquet with pavé leaves and stem. $300.00. Bottom: A pair of matching pavé frond dress clips. $750.00.

Left: Seven huge faceted rhinestones used for flower heads on sterling brooch. Ribbon has rows of smaller rhinestones. $450.00. Top: Shaped like cathedral windows, blue aquamarine glass stone petals with golden rays. Three-tiered layers. $525.00. Right: Called the Plum, has a 1" rhinestone topped with pavé leaves and a small branch. $850.00.

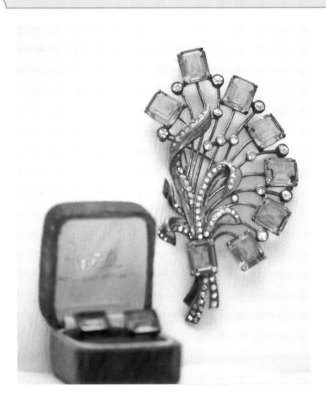

Three diamente brooches, 2½" to 3" in length. $220.00 – $300.00 each.

Eight emerald-cut topaz glass flower heads with vermeil finish. Long slender leaves have a border of small rhinestones. 4½" brooch. The earrings feature the topaz stone. $1,400.00 set.

Two diamente rhinestone ribbon bows, approximately 3½" wide. $475.00 each.

Top: Diamente ribbon bow with two ¾" emerald cut, imitation diamond rhinestones. $975.00. Bottom: Streamer pavé ribbon bow with dark red rhinestones accents. $750.00.

Three colored Original bows. Top left: Lavender rhinestones, pavé ribbon. $575.00. Top right: Pink and lavender. $550.00. Bottom: Topaz, blue, and citrine glass stones with rows of diamente. $550.00.

Left: Pear-shaped silhouette is filled with a ¾" rhinestone drop. Art Nouveau pavé leaves. $675.00. Top: Burst of gold flame accented with aquamarine crystals and topped with matching blue rhinestone. $475.00. Bottom: Sky blue rhinestones form not only the three-tiered flower but the streamers as well. Traditional Eisenberg icing of diamente ribbon makes the accents. $260.00.

Pink and red brooches and earrings, all topped with icing (diamente ribbons). Earrings, $80.00 to $95.00 pair. Brooches, $140.00 each.

Amethyst, lavender, and red rhinestones with pavé icing. Matching earrings. $450.00 set.

Three Art Nouveau brooches. All done in pavé and silverplated. $225.00 – 275.00 each.

Chemical infusion has given the blue rhinestones a pink and dark blue stripe. Brooch and matching clip-on earrings. $350.00

Left: Light and dark green rhinestones with a citrine focal point form the flower with dark green navette rhinestone leaves. Pavé, gold-plated stem. $245.00. Middle: Diamente snowflake brooch. $195.00. Right: Two-point rhinestone garlands caught by pavé ribbon. $180.00 – 195.00.

The same pink and blue stripe stone is used in this necklace and earring set. $300.00.

A trio of necklaces: Note the Eisenberg clasp. Left: Two shades of blue rhinestones with just two diamente rhinestones at each side of center drop. $180.00. Middle: Clear crystals combined with diamente rhinestones. $150.00. Right: Rich pink rhinestones form the chain. Eight perpendicular chatons clustered around a suspended drop. $225.00.

Left: Burma red, pear-shaped rhinestones petals around a clear rhinestone. Three larger pear-shaped diamente rhinestones create the backdrop and icing ribbon trim. Matching earrings. $430.00. Right: Burma red and fuchsia rhinestones form a floral bouquet tied with pavé ribbon. Matching earrings. $375.00.

Left: Sapphire blue rhinestone cluster, pavé ribbon, streamers finished with same dark blue rhinestones. $180.00 – $195.00. Right: Ice blue rhinestone brooch and earrings with pavé ribbon decor. $250.00.

Left: Pink clustered wreath with matching earrings. $325.00. Right: Circle of pink rhinestones tied with pavé ribbon has matching earrings. $295.00.

Two Eisenberg Ice brooch sets. Left: Black and white faux pearls enhanced by pavé leaves. Earrings use both colors of pearls. $180.00 – 195.00. Right: Imitation jade brooch and earrings, accented with pavé leaves. $150.00 – 165.00.

Left: Brown and amber rhinestone garlands tied with pavé ribbon. Matching earrings. $135.00 – 150.00. Middle: Amber rhinestones and diamente icing. Matching earrings. $120.00. Right: Amber and topaz rhinestones with diamente leaves. Matching earrings. $135.00 – 150.00.

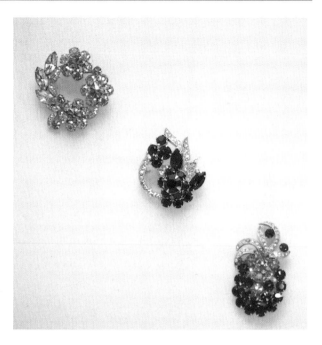

Left: Green and gold rhinestones arc, flower, and leaves with touches of pavé ribbon. Matching earrings. $120.00. Right: Citrine and topaz rhinestones, diamente icing. Matching earrings. $135.00.

Top: Pink floral circle. $125.00. Middle: Sapphire blue chaton and navette rhinestones captured by diamente frame. $150.00. Bottom: Pink and purple berry-shaped with pavé leaves and two small dark purple rhinestones. $180.00.

Left: Faberge blue enamel egg pendant and earrings. Decorated with pavé rhinestones. $395.00. Right: Aquamarine plastic parure has brooch, necklace, and earrings with streams of rhinestones (1960s). $250.00.

Left: Five-tier Christmas tree with multicolored rhinestones. $85.00. Middle: Holiday wreath with green, white, and red rhinestones. $90.00 – $105.00. Right: Art Deco tree with multicolored stones, topped with gold star. $95.00.

Artist Picasso lent his talents to these two enameled necklaces. Left: Made of white enamel with gold outlined feathers, this owl perches on a branch. $125.00. Right: Pink, lavender, red, black, and blue Impressionistic owl. $180.00.

Five holiday trees. $85.00 – 100.00.

Left: Bands of colored rhinestones alternating with diamente pavé topped with pear-shaped clear rhinestone and green rhinestone trunk. $105.00. Top: Red, green chaton rhinestones and clear navettes. $120.00. Right: Green chatons, clear pear-shaped rhinestones tree. $95.00.

3½" diamente eagle with enameled black beak, eyes, and claws. Matching earrings. $850.00.

1990s pavé spider with antennae. Body of graduated clear rhinestones. Largest one is ½". $350.00.

Left: Moth features clear crystal glass in upper wings and blue navette rhinestones in lower wings. Gold-plated body has pavé rhinestones. $135.00. Lower: Gold-plated dove has navette green crystal stones with touches of clear rhinestones. Original.$350.00. Right: Topaz faceted glass body, gold-plated wings on bug. $95.00.

Top left: Brooch with clear, citrine, and lime rhinestones. $120.00. Top right: Topaz and amber rhinestones in leaf design. $125.00 – 140.00. Middle: Citrine and champagne rhinestone brooch. $135.00. Bottom: Green two-tone rhinestones in a double circle, wrapped with pavé ribbon. $100.00.

Left: Sky blue bracelet with earrings. Pavé insert creates a bow design. $395.00. Right: Each clear navette rhinestone is bridged with a framework of small clear rhinestones. Smaller navettes link the double row. With matching earrings. $300.00.

Five bracelets. First: Double row, clear chatons, bar design is made with two chatons in between. $110.00. Second: Three rows of two sizes of clear chatons. Double locking clasp. $165.00. Third: Rich blue rhinestones with two clear special cut cross shape rhinestones. $180.00. Fourth: One row of clear rhinestones. $95.00. Fifth: Large clear chatons linked by three small clear rhinestones. $140.00.

Four pairs of pink and red rhinestone clip-on earrings. $85.00 – 100.00 pair.

Nine pairs of diamente clip-on earrings. $85.00 – 110.00 pair.

Three diamente rhinestone silver-plated rings. Left: Single large emerald cut clear rhinestone has smaller rhinestone on each side. $135.00. Middle: Ring has clear emerald cut rhinestone turned to form a diamond shape, framed with small sapphire rhinestones. $175.00. Right: Pavé diamente cocktail ring. $140.00. Top: Small diamente brooch. $95.00.

Kenneth Jay Lane

History

Began: 1963
Still in business
Designer: Kenneth J. Lane
Signed: Kenneth Lane Laguna (pearls)
Kenneth Jay Lane (Saks 5th Ave)
KJL for Avon (Avon)
K.J.L. (1963 – 1973) KJL (1974 – current)

Characteristics

Larger-than-life pieces
Deep, full-valued colors
Sold by QVC, Franklin Mint, Avon

A town better known for its automobiles than jewelry turned out a polished, elegant young man. Kenneth Jay Lane was born in Detroit, Michigan, and took advantage of the education offered by the University of Michigan as an architectural undergraduate. He soon discovered that wasn't what he wanted, and he went to Providence to attend the Rhode Island School of Design.

Graduating in 1954, Mr. Lane became a layout assistant at *Vogue* magazine which did not seem to fulfill his ambitions. Genesco gave him a job designing shoes for such clients as Christian Dior and I. Miller. First he did shoes, then shoe buckles, and finally his imagination soared on to earrings. The bold, dramatic, dangling styles were soon featured at Henri Bendel's New York store.

Taking courage in hand, Lane decided to open his own jewelry firm in 1962. Eight years out of college, he had found his heart's desire — costume jewelry designing. His first line came out in 1963 and soon became the rage of the jet set.

Using faraway places, he drew inspiration wherever he traveled, India — Japan, France, Italy, England — using striking, startling color combinations, stunning designs for larger-than-life pieces. But the colors, designs, and sizes were balanced by Lane to give women the elegance and style of jewelry that could be worn for decades.

He achieved his striking colors by special ordering his rhinestones from Germany. He wanted reds that were reds, blues that were blue, colors with depth and full-strength values.

The first ten years he used "K.J.L." as his logo trademark. The jewelry line he created for Saks Fifth Avenue was signed with his full name, Kenneth Jay Lane. The jewelry that he designed for Laguna featuring their pearls was signed Kenneth Lane Laguna.

Gloria Fiori, Bonwit Teller jewelry buyer in the 1960s, bought his early jewelry and established a friendship with young Lane. Years later when she joined Avon, Lane was invited to create for her once again, under the trademark "KJL for Avon."

His registered trademark is "Jeweler to the World's Most Admired Women." And he was — the three-strand pearl choker worn by Barbara Bush at her husband's inaugural was KJL and is now on display at the Smithsonian Institute. Jackie Onassis, Madonna, Jerry Hall, Nancy Reagan, and the Duchess of Windsor have also worn Kenneth Jay Lane jewelry proudly.

Green enamel frog parure. Gold bump spots. Brooch has hinged back lid that opens to reveal a watch. Seven frogs leap on bracelet. Earrings are on original card. $395.00.

Avon parure of necklace, earrings, and brooch. Double strand black bead necklace, clasp is two rams with rhinestone eyes. Ram earrings and brooch. $195.00 set.

Laguna double strand pearls. Pavé diamente rhinestones on clasp and earrings. $200.00 set.

Triple strand pearls. Clasp has KJL initials. $110.00.

Necklace of white chalk beads, black beads, tubes, and gold spacers. $60.00.

Avon leopard necklace and earrings. Green rhinestone eyes and earring centers. $145.00 set.

Enamel and gold-plated elephant necklace. Pavé diamente rhinestones. $130.00.

Gold-plated crown and earrings. Diamente rhinestones. $70.00.

Top: Dragonfly with enamel wings, pink rhinestone upper body. Clear rhinestone lower body. $85.00. Bottom: Pearl body flies, pink rhinestone wings. $65.00.

Gold-plated lantern brooch with pavé diamente rhinestones. Earrings have large clear rhinestone centers. $110.00.

Gold-plated bow brooch and earrings. Pavé diamente rhinestones. $98.00.

Top: Imitation blue lapis cabochon turtle with pavé diamente rhinestones. $105.00. Bottom: Imitation blue lapis cabochon ring with pavé diamente rhinestone petals. $150.00.

Hammered gold-plated parure of bracelet, brooch, and earrings. Lion door knocker brooch. Bracelet and earrings utilize the knocker for design. $285.00.

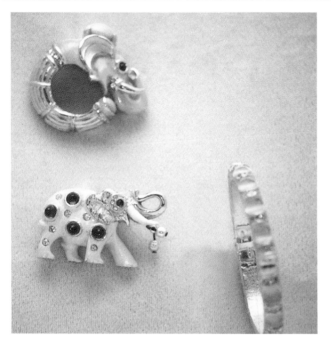

Left: Pink and blue enamel turtle brooch. $110.00. Right: Imitation coral cabochon turtle. $45.00.

Top: Enamel elephant brooch. $180.00. Bottom left: Gold-plated elephant, emerald green and clear rhinestones. Imitation ivory tusk with pearl drops. $135.00. Bottom, right: Enamel and clear rhinestone bracelet. $90.00.

Silver and gold stegosaurus, green rhinestone eyes. $135.00.

Left: Faux pearl penguin. Pavé diamente rhinestone feet, cane, beak, and hat. $85.00. Right: Gold-plated tree, green rhinestones, hang tag. $68.00. Bottom: Blue cabochon body sea horse, pavé diamente rhinestones. $85.00.

Top: Kissing fish brooch. Imitation jade bodies, pavé diamente rhinestone heads. $80.00. Bottom: Enamel body fish, green rhinestone eyes. $95.00.

Top left: Male lion, diamente rhinestone body, imitation turquoise eyes. $145.00. Top right: Enamel parrot. Clear rhinestone head, green rhinestone eyes. $80.00. Bottom: Gold hoop, pavé diamente rhinestone earrings. $55.00.

Left: gold-plated sea shell, diamente rhinestones. $78.00. Right: Gold-plated brooch, blue cabochon center stone, imitation turquoise beads, clear rhinestones. $95.00.

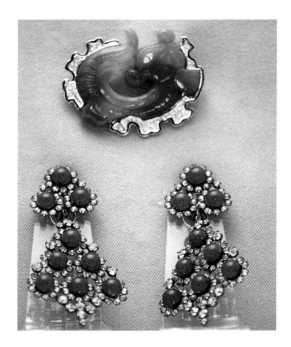

Top: Imitation jade fish. $150.00. Bottom: Imitation jade shoulder duster earrings. $175.00.

Top: Multicolored rhinestone umbrella. $55.00. Left: White glass stone Christmas tree. $45.00. Right: Opalene, green, and blue rhinestone golf bag. $68.00.

Top: Red stone top hat and cane. $40.00. Left: Rhinestone high-heeled dancing shoes trimmed in red. $45.00 each. Right: Black rhinestone top hat and cane. $40.00.

Top: Orange cabochon spider with enamel legs. $75.00. Bottom left: Diamente rhinestone spider. $80.00. Bottom right: Dark green cabochon spider with blue bead legs. $75.00.

Coiled snakes. $65.00 – 75.00.

Top: Train engine, multicolored rhinestones. $80.00. Middle: Touring car, multicolored rhinestones. $78.00. Bottom: Brightly colored rhinestone two-wheeled coach. $80.00.

Left: Rhinestone Christmas tree. $45.00. Middle: Tall tree with clear rhinestone branches decorated with many colors of rhinestones. $60.00. Right: Red and green rhinestone tree has white glass cabochons. $52.00.

Left: White and black butterfly with clear rhinestones. $75.00. Right: White butterfly with clear rhinestones. $60.00.

Top: Citrine, aurora borealis, topaz, and gold rhinestone butterfly. $110.00. Right: Three shades of blue, clear, and green rhinestone butterfly. $115.00.

Light blue, fuchsia, and dark blue crystal tree has two little rose-colored bug visitors. $98.00.

Left: Twin ram gold-plated bracelet. $80.00. Right: Dark blue center stones and pearl earrings. $40.00.

Imitation turquoise and pearls with clear rhinestones from emerald cabochon drop with clear rhinestone trim. Earrings. $210.00.

Lemon, gold, and bronze cabochons, rows of diamente rhinestones, ending in faux pearls. Earrings. $200.00.

Imitation jade and opal shoulder duster earrings. Pink and diamente rhinestones. $275.00.

Star Novelty Jewelry Co.

History

Began: 1925
Closed: 1947
Designer: Unknown
Signed: Staret

Characteristics

Eisenberg look-alikes
Eisenberg icing decoration
Oversized pieces

The Windy City, home of famous stockyards and Lakeshore Drive, also had a jewelry section of town. The Star Novelty Jewelry Company, Inc. was located in Chicago, Illinois from 1925 to 1947.

Manufacturers of rhinestone ornaments and novelty jewelry, unconfirmed rumors tell of the company's financial backing from the Eisenberg Company. The story goes on to state that Star Novelty made brooches for the Chicago-based Eisenberg.

Certainly that story seems to have some basis when you look at these pieces on display. They are oversized, with lots of high lead content glass rhinestones in the styles of Eisenberg, yet the pieces are clearly marked "Staret."

They used white metal, sometimes called pot metal, and cast designs that repeated the look of Eisenberg. Even the diamente ribbon icing was used to festoon their jewelry.

Star Novelty jewelry is marked on the surface "Staret," but the underlying impression bespeaks Eisenberg. Remember there was no copyright law in effect back then to protect anyone who wanted to manufacture their own versions of a popular selling item.

Red/white/blue enameling, diamente rhinestone and pearl brooch. $350.00.

Aquamarine rhinestone 3" brooch. $250.00.

Gold clip, diamente ribbons and leaves, gold rhinestones. $195.00.

Pearl bud flower, diamente stem and leaves. $200.00.

Burma red rhinestone fur clip. Diamente ribbon icing. $225.00.

Diamente rhinestone branch, silver-plated brooch. $190.00.

Fur clip, emerald cut rhinestones, silver-plated. $180.00.

Nosegay of three flowers made of clear chatons with emerald cut rhinestones, leaves, diamente ribbon stems, silver-plated. $190.00.

White metal brooch. $200.00.

Pavé diamente rhinestone fuchsia brooch with green faceted crystal accents. 4¼" overall height. $375.00.

Designing Men

This chapter will introduce you to four men who were trendsetters because of their ability to maintain quality, create timeless beauty, and please the fashionable women of both yesterday and today.

Yes, I said "today," for all of the designers in this chapter are highly collectible, and better yet, their designs can be worn today and still receive raves.

Study the pictures closely, sharpen your shopping skills, and you will be ready to add their work to your collection.

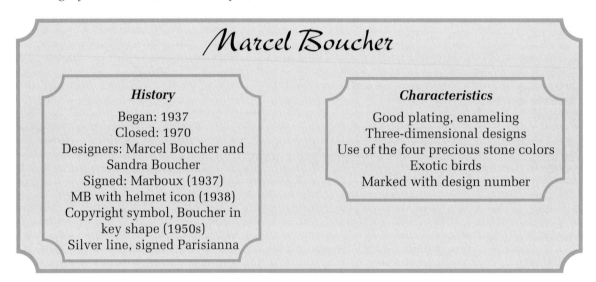

Marcel Boucher

History

Began: 1937
Closed: 1970
Designers: Marcel Boucher and
Sandra Boucher
Signed: Marboux (1937)
MB with helmet icon (1938)
Copyright symbol, Boucher in
key shape (1950s)
Silver line, signed Parisianna

Characteristics

Good plating, enameling
Three-dimensional designs
Use of the four precious stone colors
Exotic birds
Marked with design number

Frenchman Marcel Boucher came to the United States as a young man in 1925. His craftsmanship and natural French talent for discerning fine fashion helped him to become a jewelry designer for Cartier, one of the finest jewelry companies in New York City where he polished his skills in the fine jewelry trade.

From elegant brooches, he went to shoe buckles, creating them for Mazer Company during the early 1930s. In 1937 he struck out on his own with the trademark "Marboux."

Working hard, he created a line featuring six bird pins. But oh, what birds, birds that almost put Mother Nature's handiwork to shame — birds of imagination, ornate with colored stones, bright enamels, three-dimensional, ready to soar. With birds in hand, he went to Saks Fifth Avenue and made his first sale, a $20,000 order during the Depression, equivalent to winning a gold medal at the International World Olympics.

He and a partner quickly developed a working pattern that allowed him to design and the partner to handle the models and sales.

The line was also marked "MB" with a stylized helmet, the Phrygian cap worn during the French Revolution. Some collectors called the symbol a hawk or rooster icon. Boucher's company was producing 30 to 40 designs weekly. New lines were brought out twice a year, with over 300 designs created year after year.

No wonder he developed the practice of assigning design numbers to each piece. His unique practice of etching the design number of three or four digits into master models made the number a permanent identification and a tip for the collector looking for a Boucher piece. His jewelry was noted for its quality and stones of outstanding color.

In 1940 the trademark MB was used. In the 1950s, the company began to use the copyright symbol along with the name "Boucher," plus the design number which was stamped separately on the piece. The year 1940 brought about a fling in Mexican silver, sold under the name "Parisianna."

In 1947, France lost another fine jewelry craftsman to America when Sandra came to the U. S. Having had extensive training in fine jewelry, Sandra chose to learn about the United States costume jewelry industry and for nine years worked at Boucher.

She went on to become the head designer at Tiffany, but her charming smile haunted her old boss, and in 1960, the two were wed. Five years of marriage were celebrated before Marcel died in 1965.

The experience of working with Marcel gave Sandra the courage to take on the tremendous task of carrying on the Boucher name.

The offices and manufacturing facilities of the Boucher Company were located in East Toronto, Canada.

She continued in the business five years after Marcel's death before selling to Davorn Industries in 1970. Examine closely the following pictures that reveal the creative artistry that was interwoven and strengthened by the hands of Marcel and Sandra.

Gold-plated lyre bird, wings of polished gold and diamente pavé breast and head. The tree bears faux pearls. $375.00.

Gold-plated, green and blue rhinestones stud wings and tail. Bird has pavé breast and head feathers. Green eye. $300.00 – 350.00.

Faux turquoise breasted cockatiel perches on golden limb. Ruffled diamente pavé collar. $260.00.

Sapphire blue rhinestones on the body and upper wings. Large tail accented with two pavé diamente feathers in the middle. The head is a large lighter blue rhinestone. $300.00.

Pair of resting butterflies. Bottom one is black and gold. Upper is diamente rhinestones perched on a spring base, a trembler. $280.00.

Pastel blue plastic, veined petals on silver-plated brooch and matching earrings. Marked "Marboux." $135.00.

Top left: A burst of diamente rhinestones is achieved by using both chatons and baguettes. $95.00. Top right: Twin pavé diamente blossoms with faux pearl centers have stem of channeled baguettes. $105.00. Bottom: Row of diamente pavé chatons is crisscrossed with a row of baguettes in clip-back earrings. Can be worn with either brooch. $78.00.

Art Nouveau sweep uses a combination of diamente baguette and chaton rhinestones in brooch. The ear hoops have twin designs at the top and a smaller one at the bottom. $225.00.

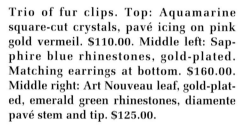

Trio of fur clips. Top: Aquamarine square-cut crystals, pavé icing on pink gold vermeil. $110.00. Middle left: Sapphire blue rhinestones, gold-plated. Matching earrings at bottom. $160.00. Middle right: Art Nouveau leaf, gold-plated, emerald green rhinestones, diamente pavé stem and tip. $125.00.

Top: Sapphire blue rhinestones, gold-plated fur clip. $130.00. Bottom left: Clip-on earrings with sapphire blue rhinestones. $70.00. Bottom middle and right: Brooch with matching earrings, diamente-tipped gold feather. $115.00.

Top and bottom left: Dark red rhinestone dahlia brooch and earrings. $180.00. Bottom middle and right: Red enamel holly berries, green enamel leaves, gold-plated. $140.00.

Left: Art Deco sapphire blue and diamente rhinestone square brooch and matching earrings below. $175.00. Right: Twin gold-plated fur clips with diamente rhinestone accents, matching earrings below. $160.00.

Floral brooch and earrings feature gray pearl flower buds and pavé diamente rhinestones. Earrings also have two faux white pearls. $225.00.

Two ribbon brooches. Top left: Entwined red and clear rhinestones. $120.00. Top right: Looped twin clear baguette rhinestone ribbons. $95.00. Bottom: Diamente pavé rhinestone ear hoops. $98.00.

Pastel moonstones. Top left: Three diamente pavé rhinestones with blue moonstone centers. $95.00. Top right: Long stem of clear baguette rhinestones and six blue moonstone petals. $80.00. Bottom: Pink moonstone earrings with pavé diamente leaves. $60.00.

Top left: Gold-plated bud earring has a ring of sapphire blue rhinestones with a red cabochon center. $65.00. Bottom left: Pair of pearl and gold earrings. $45.00. Left center: Long-stemmed, gold-plated flower has faux pearl center encircled with red rhinestones. $60.00. Right center: Gold-plated bow with pavé diamente rhinestones in the inner curve. $85.00. Top right: Matching earring to one on the left. Bottom right: Matching clip-on earrings of blue and diamente rhinestones. $75.00.

Five strand light green pearl and clear bead necklace. $55.00.

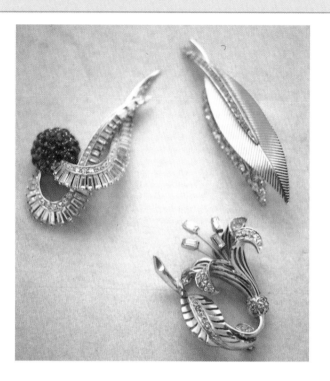

Left: Clear baguettes and chatons end in a ball of red rhinestones. $105.00. Right: Gold-plated leaf with pavé diamente rib almost conceals second diamente leaf. $80.00. Bottom: Exotic gold-plated flower, pistils with clear rhinestones. $200.00.

Left: Gold-plated ribbon bracelet encrusted with red and green cabochons and clear rhinestones, tied in a knot. $180.00. Middle: Antique gold and faux pearl link bracelet. $110.00. Right: Gold-plated watch marked "Boucher." $150.00.

Top: Sea anemone, gold-plated, touched with clear rhinestones and a cluster of small seed pearls in center. $165.00. Bottom: Gold-plated coral branches surround a center ball of clear rhinestones. $130.00.

Left: Matching earrings and bracelet done in gold plating with blood red rhinestones. $170.00. Right: Ornate gold-plated necklace has center design of clear and red rhinestones. Red rhinestones enhance the curve of the entire necklace. $110.00.

Display of Boucher imitation precious stones designs. Top left: Butterfly wings have imitation diamond, ruby, sapphire, and emerald rhinestones. Turquoise used in body. $135.00. Top right: A circular feather mound around one pearl. $90.00. Bottom, left: Knot of sapphire, ruby, and emerald rhinestones. $105.00. Bottom right: Wreath of the four imitation precious stones (rhinestones). $110.00.

Left: Same design as sea anemone at top left on page 39 with a center of faux turquoise beads. $165.00. Right: Two fuchsia and one topaz faceted crystals, gold-plated, scattered clear rhinestones. $280.00.

Top: Brooch has recessed blue moonstones in a field of gold burrs and clear rhinestones. $90.00. Bottom left: Vermeil wash with emerald green baguette rhinestones brooch. $155.00. Bottom right: Gold-Plated dahlia, alternating rows of petals of gold cut-work or clear rhinestones. $125.00.

Older enamel brooch. Ruby and aquamarine crystal blossom. 4½" tall, rhodium-plated. $425.00.

Left: Bracelet, gold-plated, red cabochons, gold cut-work. $80.00. Right: Bracelet, five links with orange cabochon centers framed with gold filigree metal work. $90.00.

Ring and matching earrings feature large faux pearls. Gold-plated seaweed cradles them. $145.00.

Left: Christmas angel with green enameled garland, red rhinestone berries. $85.00. Right: Enamel tropical fish. $68.00.

Left: Enamel beaked bird, gold-plated, pearl egg. $85.00. Right: Enamel, gold-plated starfish. $55.00.

Left: Antique silver pewter finish owl. $80.00. Right: Antique silver pewter finish snarling cat. $95.00.

Left: Enameled fish, head and fin edges of small rhinestones. $80.00. Middle: Gold-plated pirate's chest filled with glass imitation stones. $78.00. Right: Enameled leaf with ribs of clear rhinestones. $58.00.

Castlecliff Jewelry Inc.

History

Began: 1937
Closed: 1977
Designer: William Markle
Signed: Castlecliff 1940 – 1954
Castlecliff with copyright symbol
Castlemark

Characteristics

Bold, intricate designs
Three-dimensional
Tremblers
Well-constructed
Gold-plated

Clifford Furst introduced his Castlecliff line to the better department stores in 1945. He incorporated his first name into his trademark along with the word "castle," a prediction that his line would be royally fit for one who would live in a castle.

Since he was in operation from 1937 into the 1970s, you'll find the Castlecliff cartouche without the copyright mark on his earlier pieces. The last 15 years of his production, the company used the copyright symbol protecting its designs.

Castlemark was another trademark registered to Clifford Furst. Designs were reflective of history and came from all over the world, especially highlighting Aztec and Chinese flavors.

Chief designer William Markle drew on his architectural background to create bold, intricate, well-constructed Gothic, Renaissance, and Art Deco costume jewelry.

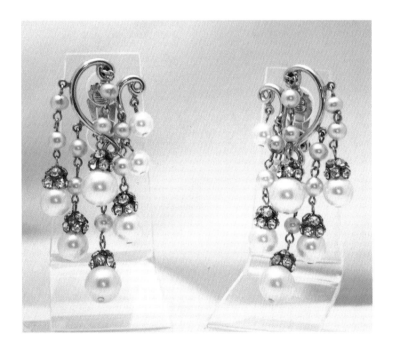

Gold-plated clip-on earrings, 2¾" from top to bottom and 1½" wide. Five 1½" drops cascade at spaced intervals. Each drop has two small faux pearls, rhinestone caps on one large pearl at the bottom. Two small pearls drop from inner curve of earring base. $125.00 – 145.00.

Thistle blossom, 3" long, 2" wide, 2" high, each stalk japanned, ending in a fitting that accommodates light and dark blue rhinestones. Top is a large, dark green chaton (15mm). Stem is wired onto a gold-plated, open work branch. $375.00 – 450.00.

The simplicity of this gold-plated brooch allows three 25mm iridescent blue faceted rhinestones to command the design. Earrings each have a blue single rhinestone. $160.00 – 180.00.

Sterling crown, 1¾" wide by 2" tall, open facade. Three pearl top ornaments, ruby-red rhinestones with diamente accents. $170.00.

Art Nouveau 2" brooch. Three golden leaves cap the green pear-shaped cabochon hanging from the branch. One long leaf with three small ones that are heavily veined. $45.00 – 60.00.

Left: "Castlemark" logo is on 1¼" domed brooch with tic-tic-toe outline done in baguettes. Diamente rhinestones for formal wear. $55.00. Right: Silver-plated, 2¼" brooch. Three dimensional branches with bark finish surround a bundle of stemmed, diamente flowers. $115.00 – 130.00.

2" circle pin. Golden maple leaves provide a base for kidney-shaped green cabochons; small green cabochons; green, yellow, and diamente faceted glass; dark green rhinestones. $125.00 – 145.00.

Left: A golden laurel wreath fit for Caesar is encrusted with nine faux pearls. $40.00. Right: Golden porcupine with braided gold quills. $50.00.

Oriental silver-plated necklace, 14" long, 6" design features two bows, 3¼" wide by 1¾" high, connected by a Chinese character, ending with a 1¾" triangle. $90.00.

Hinged cuff bracelet, 1½" wide with special locking keeper. Design is two, ⅝" wide textured, curved bands with individually set diamente rhinestones in a row girdling the middle. $125.00 – 145.00.

Golden jungle cat, hinged cuff bracelet. Animal skin textured to resemble fur and polished in certain areas to show dots. Full, detailed head with green rhinestone eyes. Band ¾" wide, at the head 1½" wide. $175.00 – 250.00.

Left: Winking cat, 1¼" tall with golden head, one green rhinestone eye. $30.00 – 40.00. Middle: Quail, 1½" long by 1" wide, enameled with golden accents, green rhinestone eye. $45.00. Right: Antelope, 1¾" tall, enamel head, blue cabochon body. $30.00 – 35.00.

Gold-plated fish with scales of golden burrs carries a faux pearl in his mouth. Polished and satin finishes and green rhinestone eyes. $85.00.

Trembler brooch. Butterfly mounted on a spring hovers over the gold leaf and pavé wings. 2" overall. $125.00.

Left: Markle's version of the pea pod. Gold-plated finish is lightly scored with small burrs and contains seven small, faux pearls. $85.00 – 125.00. Right: Gold-plated, 2½" brooch with polished and satin finishes on four petals and a 1" center. Seven smoky rhinestones outline each petal. $65.00.

Faux turquoise, lapis, jade, and carnelian stones in Aztec theme necklace and earrings. $175.00.

Christian Dior

History

Began: 1930
Still in business
Designers: Christian Dior
Roger Scermame
Henry Schreiner
Signed: Christian Dior
Dior West Germany (year date)
Christian Dior by Kramer, 1950 – 1957
Christian Dior in oval 1958 to present

Characteristics

Fashion designer jewelry
Limited quantity production
First to use aurora borealis rhinestones

We have the French people to thank for nurturing Christian Dior. He was born in 1905 in a country that bequeathed an artistic flair and the appreciation for fine style. This native Frenchman's attributes made it a natural instinct for him to turn to the art world where he established an excellent business record as an art dealer.

His love of beauty took him that one step farther when he became an apprentice at several different Parisian fashion houses. It didn't take long for this talented man to open the House of Dior and in 1947, he received the fashion world's accolades for his new designs, bringing back into style the feminine look.

From 1930 to 1955 Mitchell Maer held the jewelry license for Dior jewelry. Of course, Dior wanted to dress his famous clients from head to toe, so jewelry and other accessories were selected to compliment his fashion line.

In 1950 Dior licensed the United States' production of his jewelry to Kramer of New York. Kramer was awarded the privilege of putting his American firm's name on the Dior jewelry and proudly marked each piece that he produced for Dior.

The Grosse family, a famous German jewelry firm, was licensed in 1955 to manufacture the jewelry. The firm. Henkel and Grosse, marked their pieces "Dior West Germany" and placed the year of manufacture along with the name.

Unfortunately, the world lost Dior in 1957 but he left his legacy — the House of Dior. Yves St. Laurent, who had been Dior's apprentice, continued producing the jewelry marked with Dior's name that can be found in boutiques today. Beginning in 1958, the jewelry was stamped with an oval enclosing the name Christian Dior.

3½" gold-plated bird. Two sizes of ruby cabochons, rimmed with rhinestones of dusty rose and dark blue rhinestones. $200.00.

Gold-plated brooch, pear-shaped diamente rhinestones. $225.00.

Gold-plated chain with diamente rhinestone framing faceted dark blue crystal. $295.00

Golden insect with dark green eyes on bar pin. $15.00.

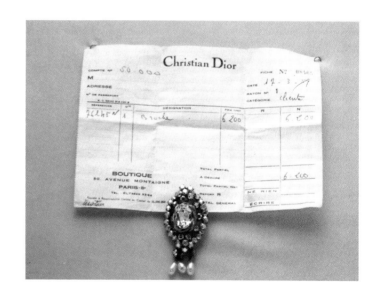

Brooch with original Paris, France, bill of sale noted in francs. Aurora borealis rhinestones around a citrine crystal with three seed pearl drops. $400.00.

Gold-plated rose. $180.00.

Imitation ruby, sapphire, and diamond rhinestones with faux pearls. $450.00.

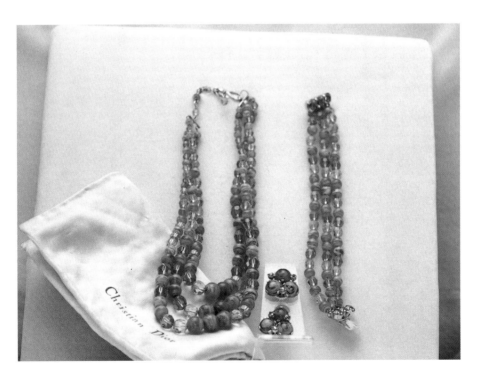

Christian Dior presentation cloth accompanies parure of necklace, bracelet, and earrings. Heavy glass earthtone beads. Triple strand necklace and bracelet. $650.00.

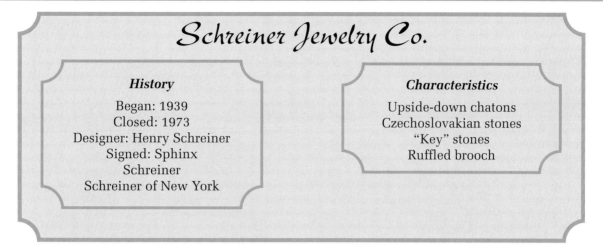

Schreiner Jewelry Co.

History

Began: 1939
Closed: 1973
Designer: Henry Schreiner
Signed: Sphinx
Schreiner
Schreiner of New York

Characteristics

Upside-down chatons
Czechoslovakian stones
"Key" stones
Ruffled brooch

Henry Schreiner immigrated to the United States from Bavaria, Germany, in 1923 and held several odd jobs to tide himself over. There wasn't much opportunity to use his German trade of blacksmithing in New York City until he discovered the Better Buckle Company where his metal-working talents served him well. The company was fortunate to have found him, for his skills helped him create some outstanding shoe buckles.

Accessorizing for the garment industry allowed him an outlet for his artistic and creative sides as well. Belt buckles, buttons, and dress fasteners gave him an opportunity to acquire fashion design training on the job.

In 1951, daughter Terry joined her father, bringing with her a talented husband, Ambros Albert, to the Schreiner business. Soon the threesome was creating jewelry for Adele Simpson, Norman Norell, and Christian Dior. When designing for his special fashion clientele, Schreiner would never place his name on the jewelry.

Only jewelry made for retail store sales was marked with the firm name "Schreiner" or "Schreiner of New York." Top models wore his bib necklaces, colored baroque brooches, large pendants, and dangling earrings down many fashion runways.

Henry had kept his ties with the old country, and he was able to get custom-made stones for his thriving company. He had key stones made in Germany by skilled Czechoslovakian craftsmen. These rhinestones are a special shape, long and slender, wider at the top, then tapering down, almost the shape of an old-fashioned keyhole. The stones were very expensive, exclusive for Schreiner, and are no longer manufactured. So it is very important to take good care of his jewelry.

Another Schreiner trademark technique was crystal chatons inserted upside down. The tabletop-smooth surface of the faceted stone was now underneath, picking up the color of the garment being worn. The pointed bottom of the stone was now on top to catch the light.

Although Henry died in 1954, Schreiner's standards of handwork and unusual designs were carried on by his daughter and son-in-law. During all the years they were in business, Schreiner never mass produced their jewelry. The firm closed their operations in 1973.

Imitation coral necklace and earrings. $225.00.

Black and white glass cabochon necklace and earrings.
$150.00.

Gun metal finish necklace. Red, pink, and diamente rhinestones. $300.00.

Bronze and smoky rhinestone brooch and
earrings. $245.00.

Glass cabochon, blue novelty glass stones, pink and
green rhinestone brooch and earrings. $295.00.

Citrine crystal and diamente rhinestone brooch and earrings. $280.00.

Frosted pink and white cabochons and pink rhinestone brooch and earrings. $195.00.

Dark brown, red, gold, and silver rhinestone brooch. $110.00.

Citrine glass upside-down chaton (pointed end is now on top) and gold rhinestone brooch and earrings. $350.00.

Key cut citrine stones and olive green crystal brooch and earrings. $305.00.

Golden starburst brooch with large glass center. $145.00.

Left: Glass, novelty stone brooch. $85.00. Right: Gold flower, metallic rhinestones. $90.00.

Left: Pale and dark blue cabochons, blue and clear rhinestone brooch. $105.00. Right: Imitation turquoise stones, dark blue cabochons, metallic rhinestone brooch. $145.00.

Emerald cut crystal brooch. $280.00.

Left: Faux pearl, blue rhinestones and bead brooch. $80.00. Right: Faux coral and turquoise brooch. $110.00.

Black rhinestone flower. $110.00.

Traveling snail, brown and aurora borealis rhinestones. $135.00

Faux pearl, aurora borealis rhinestone bug. $80.00.

Top: Special effect pink cabochon and pink rhinestone brooch. $185.00. Bottom: Purple dome earrings. $70.00.

Designing Women

Of course, we must give equal time to the women who set fashion trends, women who designed not only jewelry pieces but also the complete costume.

They dressed the women of America, France, and Italy from head to toe, and the rest of the fashion world followed. Fabric was purchased by the bolts, nimble seamstresses brought to reality the paper designs. Loose rhinestones tumbled into bins and manufacturers turned out the jewelry to be worn on these creations. Here is the jewelry — oh, wouldn't it be wonderful to see the complete costume!

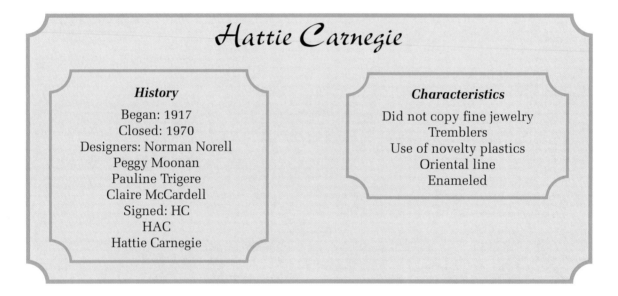

Hattie Carnegie

History

Began: 1917
Closed: 1970
Designers: Norman Norell
Peggy Moonan
Pauline Trigere
Claire McCardell
Signed: HC
HAC
Hattie Carnegie

Characteristics

Did not copy fine jewelry
Tremblers
Use of novelty plastics
Oriental line
Enameled

Vienna, Austria, was the birthplace for Hattie Kanengeister in 1886. She came to America in 1902 as a six-year-old where her last name was changed to Carnegie.

She had to leave school at the age of ten to go to work to help her widowed mother make ends meet for the family. She found employment at Macy's as a messenger girl then became a pin girl in the millinery workroom, advancing to an assistant in a dress house.

The hard work and time spent behind the scenes of the garment industry served her well. At the age of 23 she was ready to show the world what she could do. Friend Rose Roth, a seamstress, joined her in forming a business in which Hattie would design hats and Rose would sew garments.

This messenger girl, with little formal education, would go on to build an $8,000,000 fashion industry in her 59 years of business. She did not copy fine jewelry in her costume designs despite the trend to do so, and avoided creating any piece that could be mistaken for a jewelry store purchase.

Her jewelry incorporated plastics, enamel, and gold-plated finishes with rhinestones as accents only. Her tremblers, in earlier days called nodders, fascinated the public. Each design incorporated tiny springs that gave movement to specific parts of the jewelry when the wearer moved. Each delicate sigh or breath would cause the flowers of a brooch to nod. A slight movement of the head would cause the earrings to vibrate and tremble.

A magnificent butterfly, shown on page 58, was so large that she chose to suspend it from two points by chains, creating a stunning necklace. The purple cabochons fill the wings, and yet the delicate open work design provokes the notion that the butterfly had flown into her design studio. To me, there has always been an unsolved mystery connected with this piece of costume jewelry — for what dress was it designed? What Carnegie creation was graced by this butterfly accessory?

After her death in 1956, the jewelry line was sold to Larry Josephs who remained in business until 1970.

Faux diamond and pearls parure consisting of necklace, bracelet, and clip-on earrings. Rhodium-plated. $575.00.

Opera length necklace using aurora borealis and fuchsia beads along with small rich green beads. Matching earrings. $190.00.

Double strand necklace of frosted topaz beads and blue aurora borealis beads has large frosted topaz glass cabochon. Beads are also used in five drops. Matching trefoil drop earrings. $375.00

Ten strand necklace of crystal beads. $110.00.

The magnificent 7" wide by 4½" tall butterfly necklace. $750.00.

4" x 3½" articulated elephant. $350.00.

5" floral brooch and earrings. Gold-plated, blue and black rhinestones. $390.00.

Trembler (nodder) floral brooch and matching earrings. Matte gold finish and large clear rhinestones.
Each flower head is mounted on tiny springs.
$450.00.

Trembler, silver-plated. White moonstones,
blue rhinestones. Brooch and earrings.
$525.00.

Left: Tourmaline rhinestones in crescent brooch
with matching earrings. $275.00. Right: Blue plastic
filament centers, circled with gold-plated frame.
Brooch and earrings. $150.00.

Left: Brooch, matching earrings below. Enameled flower
with sapphire blue rhinestone circled with clear rhinestones. $125.00. Top middle: Gold-plated brooch with auro-
ra borealis rhinestones. $80.00. Bottom middle: Pill box
topped with tropical fish that has enamel stripes. $95.00.
Right: Christmas tree with aurora borealis beads. $78.00.

Left: Gold-plated wheat stalks studded with clear rhinestones. $90.00. Right: Brooch features amethyst, citrine, blue, and lavender rhinestones with metallic cabochons. $145.00.

Left: Large green cabochon stone center, gold-plated leaves and accents of clear rhinestones on brooch. $115.00. Right: Brooch with dome green cabochon stone center, circle of green beads and navette rhinestones. Four pinched gold findings with special cut dark green glass stones. $180.00.

Left: Brooch with enamel flower with pearl centers on gold braid wreath with green rhinestones. $85.00. Right: Blue faux turquoise butterfly. $98.00.

Top: Faux pearl, enameled flower brooch. $115.00. Bottom and right: The green doily accompanies the pink enamel floral bouquet to form a brooch. $225.00.

Top: Faux pearl center, japanned finish loops studded with clear rhinestones. $80.00. Bottom, left and right: Three different pairs of faux pearl earrings. $35.00 – 50.00 pair.

Vintage dimensional flower of clear rhinestones. Marked HC in a diamond. $350.00.

Cameo brooch, gold-plated. $110.00. Right: Six-spoke, gold-plated, clear rhinestone center brooch. $68.00. Bottom: Single flower brooch, gold-plated, turquoise bud, pink pear-shaped rhinestones outlined in clear rhinestones. $125.00.

Top: Plastic tomato with section lines of clear rhinestones. $195.00. Bottom left: Opalene drop earrings. $90.00. Bottom middle: White milk glass cuff bracelet. $75.00. Bottom right: Red and purple earrings. $50.00.

Top: Gold-plated medallion with green glass cabochon. Rimmed with red rhinestones. $130.00. Middle: Gold-plated, braided and clear rhinestone earrings. $40.00. Bottom: Large citrine crystal earrings. $45.00.

Top: Brooch with pavé diamente rhinestones and emerald green baguettes brooch. $225.00. Bottom: Clear imitation diamond earrings. $55.00.

Left: Pink plastic center dome with gold-plated fronds. $65.00. Middle: Japanned brooch with honey and bronze cabochons. $50.00. Right: Brooch has green glass cabochons of various shapes and sizes with rust-colored ones tucked in between and accented with clear rhinestones. $78.00.

Silver-plated lion with full mane and red glass ball. $260.00.

Left: Gold-plated wreath, green and red cabochons. $85.00. Right: Gold-plated dancing cats with clear rhinestone collars. $195.00.

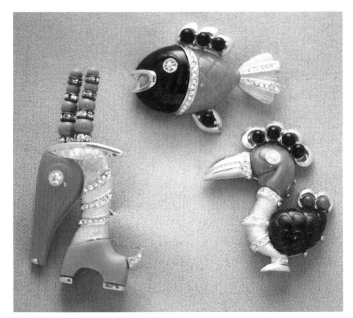

Plastic whimsicals. Left: Prongs have turquoise beads and rhinestone rondels. Gold-plated animal, has rhinestone necklace. $145.00. Top: Navy blue and rose fish with blue cabochons and clear rhinestones. $130.00. Right: Green and navy blue rooster with diamente pavé rhinestones. $110.00.

Left: Gold-plated trembler bug with clear rhinestone trim. $95.00. Right: Gold-plated lady bug with rhinestone head. $85.00. Middle: Gold-plated dragonfly, coral lower wings. $100.00.

Left: Chinese medicine man, silver-plated. $235.00. Right: Gold-plated junk with sailor, faux jade sail and waves. $255.00.

Left: Japanned burro with black enameling with pink rhinestone eyes carries pink and blue beads. $175.00. Right: Gold-plated zebra with rhinestone stripes. $195.00. Bottom: Clear yellow plastic dog with gold-plated ears and neck. $110.00.

Ring and earring set of long-horned plastic sheep. Faux coral and turquoise, clear rhinestones. $200.00.

Coco Chanel

History

Began: 1912
Still in business
Designer: Coco Chanel
Signed: Chanel

Characteristics

Entwined back-to-back Cs
Faux pearls
Ropes and chains
Bold, massive jewelry
Military flavor

There is one category of jewelry designers that can truly be called fashion designers, people who have a definite costume in mind that will be enhanced by the addition of jewelry accessories. Perhaps the costume design only existed on paper until the breath of life was given to it by the sparkling rhinestones.

Coco Chanel knew the true meaning of the complete costume and was the trend setter when she used rhinestone jewelry to accessorize her runway fashions at the Chanel Modes in Paris. An astute business woman, she realized that a woman coming into her dress salon would need shoes, hat, purse, and all the finishing touches for her new outfit.

Gabrielle Chanel was born in France in 1883 and was raised in a convent. The schooling she received there developed her fine eye for details, ability to do complicated hand sewing projects, appreciation for quality, and a dedication to achieving her goals.

She made her living as a seamstress and hat designer in Paris, saving her earrings and acquiring a following that allowed her to open her own shop, Chanel Modes, in 1912.

Her petite frame adorned by her own designs with arms ringed with bracelets drew attention when Coco mingled with the French high society. The little woman with big fashions was the darling of the rich and famous.

Couture dress designs were completed with jewelry that incorporated rows and rows of faux pearls and an abundance of ropes and chains; Chanel also favored cross motifs. Her bold jewelry made a statement for the well-dressed French woman. Her initials, CC, were placed back-to-back and featured prominently on all her accessories.

She even bottled her favorite scent, naming it Chanel #5 since she was born on August 5, and it became an instant success. A woman could shop her boutique for everything from the top of her head to the shoes on her feet, a trend-setting French retail approach. By 1938 Chanel employed over 4,000 people in her numerous houses of fine fashion.

About that time those fashions began to change, taking on a definite military flavor as if she anticipated the winds of war that were to sweep Europe.

World War II saw the closing of Chanel's doors for 15 years. Chanel Modes reopened in 1954 where she again held court for the fashion world until her death in 1971.

Chanel boutiques are still carrying on the Chanel tradition. Vintage Chanel costume jewelry is hard to find, thus making it very desirable to a collector.

Bracelet with two monogram medallions. $100.00.

Hand-painted, floral spray with red rhinestones. $375.00.

Gold-plated female portrait, pink rhinestone in check and on hat, clear rhinestone trim. $650.00.

Hand-painted, enameled trio of white flowers with blue veins and rhinestone centers. $450.00.

Hand-painted twin pastel blooms with clear rhinestone trim. $375.00.

Gold-plated turkey, pavé diamente head and wings. $525.00.

Navy blue chunky bangle with multicolored cabochons. $350.00.

Schiaparelli

History

Began: 1934
Still in business
Designers: Elsa Schiaparelli
Jean Schlumberger
Serge Matta

Characteristics

Shocking pink color
Coppola et Toppa beadwork
Crystal roses
Tourmaline rhinestones
Chunky bracelets

Coco Chanel's arch rival Elsa Schiaparelli was born in Rome, Italy, in 1890. Schiaparelli flare for life was ignited by the time she spent in the Greenwich Village section of New York. Her love of colors was developed during that "surrealist" period. Elsa was a film-script writer and at one time, a translator for an American firm doing business with Italy. The early 1920s saw her move to France where she designed fine jewelry in Paris. Now she had colors and jewelry — the next step was to open her own fashion house in Paris in 1934.

Within the year she was selling perfume, cosmetics, lingerie, swimsuits, and jewelry to compliment her fashionable line of clothing. In 1947, an age where brown, blue, and basic black were fashionable colors, she invented a pink that shocked the public and vitalized the fashion world. Shocking pink would become the trademark of Schiaparelli.

She incorporated bold, full colors in stylish jackets and short coats. She developed a liking for native African art which quickly became part of her jewelry designs. The jungle primitive was a natural for the free-thinking woman who went on to introduce jacketed evening dresses, unusual colored furs, and evening sweaters.

Many speculations were made about the rivalry between Schiaparelli and Chanel. Was it Italy versus France? Or a younger woman versus an older one (Schiaparelli was seven years younger)? A later arrival in the fashion world (Chanel had been in business for 20 years when Schiaparelli appeared)? Or was it just newspapers making copy? Perhaps it was a combination that gave each woman more press coverage that certainly helped to build both businesses.

Schiaparelli was the first to offer ready-to-wear garments in her large Place Vendome fashion house. There were 98 rooms in the establishment that housed over 350 seamstresses and fashion assistants at the peak of her business in 1940. Her top jewelry designer, Jean Schlumberger, later became the vice president of Tiffany. Italian designer Serge Matta had the Italian company of Coppola et Toppo producing jewelry for Schiaparelli.

American production of Schiaparelli began in 1949 by the Ralph DeRosa Company. At the same time she opened a branch in New York City selling her designs. In 1954 she ended her designing career and spent her final days in Paris, France, where she died in 1973.

Her jewelry is still being produced and can be found in fine boutiques.

Grand parure of necklace, brooch, earrings, ring, and bracelet. Features tourmaline crystal with gold-plated framing and green crystal beads. $625.00.

Tourmaline parure with necklace, earrings, and two bracelets. $450.00.

Pink rose crystal necklace and earrings. $330.00.

Gold-plated necklace and earrings, pavé diamente rhinestones. $210.00.

Blue crackle glass cabochons with aurora borealis navette necklace and earrings. $280.00.

Triple strand blue and green bead necklace and earrings. $190.00.

Multicolored novelty glass stone necklace and bracelet. $160.00.

Silver-plated leaf necklace. $105.00.

Double strand black bead necklace with gold balls and four long decorative tassels. $200.00.

Opalene navette brooch and earrings. Black and aurora borealis rhinestones. $125.00.

Carnival glass navettes and pearl brooch and earrings. $148.00.

Top: Gold-plated brooch with diamente rhinestones. $95.00. Middle: Crackle glass cabochons, aurora borealis rhinestones. Brooch. $110.00. Bottom: Three pairs of earrings. $55.00 – 70.00 pair.

Left: Purple cabochons, silver-plated brooch. $250.00. Right: Silver-plated brooch with purple cabochons and blue rhinestone accents. $235.00.

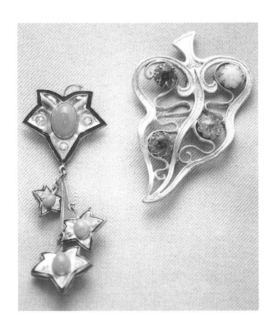

Left: Imitation coral cabochons in a grape leaf cluster. $110.00. Right: Imitation glass stones, leaf brooch. $80.00.

Gold and brown rhinestones, three drop brooch. $180.00.

Citrine and blue rhinestone earrings and bracelet. $160.00.

Silver-plated bracelet and earrings, blue rhinestone flowers. $180.00.

Pink glass cabochons, gold leaf bracelet and earrings. $135.00.

Antique gold finish bracelet and earrings in fall tones. $145.00.

Bracelet with opalene and pink glass cabochons with dark pink rhinestones. $155.00.

Left: Tourmaline bracelet. $110.00. Right: Purple cabochon bracelet. $155.00.

Aurora borealis rhinestones, purple cabochon bracelet. $125.00.

Left: Green rhinestones and cabochon bracelet. $115.00. Right: Round cream-colored cabochon bracelet. $85.00.

Left: Pink rhinestone floweret bracelet. $95.00. Right: Black finish bracelet with clear rhinestones. $140.00.

Three pairs of earrings. $80.00 – 90.00 pair. Bottom left: Gold pillbox with diamente rhinestone hearts. $95.00.

Miriam Haskell

History

Began: 1927
Still in business
Designers: Frank Hess
Larry Yverba
Signed: Miriam Haskell inside rainbow,
1940 – 1940
Miriam Haskell in oval, 1938 to present

Characteristics

Antique Russian gold finish
Tiny seed pearls
Brass wire and stampings
Findings wired together
Hand-set stones
Pin-backs never opened more than ¾"

A name that you will hear frequently aficionados is Miriam Haskell. Once you become familiar with her jewelry, you'll be able to identify it from across the room. Miriam Haskell was born in Indiana in the last year of the nineteenth century. By the time she was 26, she was running a gift shop in the McAlpine Hotel. It was 1924, and the shop was located on Herald Square, quite an accomplishment for a newcomer to New York City.

Her custom-made jewelry was bringing repeat customers, and more space was required. Her elegant artistic talents produced the sketches for the jewelry designs, but Frank Hess made them a reality. Haskell was now ready to leave the retail business and go into wholesale production.

At that time Hess was the sole designer for Haskell, but she supervised the production line. Many of their very early costume pieces before 1930 were unmarked.

Each piece was carefully hand assembled, every bead selected for its position in the design. Tiny seed pearls and soft gilding bound with delicate brass wire took the skill of fine craftsmen. Haskell had the ability to use Bakelite, turquoise, wood, leather, shells, faux pearls, and coral in massive amounts. Despite the numerous layers of beads on each piece, she maintained a balance and flow of design that made each piece a stunning fashion accessory.

An antique Russian gold metal finish was developed by Haskell and Hess that used a galvanizing bath to fuse gold and silver on a copper and brass base. This gave the metal jewelry fitting a soft antique finish, a perfect background for her special faux pearls.

The technique of embroidery with a fine brass wire was used to sew the strands of beads onto the fittings to achieve the layering in the antique look but was oh, so fragile. Each ornate clasp is an exam-

ple of this artistry. Time takes its toll on the brass and copper, so anyone brave enough to risk wearing Haskell jewelry for display may pay the price by losing rare, antique, irreplaceable beads or pearls.

Morris Kinsler bought the business in 1954 with Frank Hess remaining as designer to carry on the Haskell tradition. In 1984 Sanford Moss took over the ownership for six years.

The business sold again in 1990 to Frank Fialkoff, and the Haskell tradition of quality and originality continues today.

Imitation jade bead parure of opera length necklace, brooch, earrings, and bracelet. $475.00.

Three strand necklace and bracelet. Two shades of blue and crystal beads. Typical Haskell clasp on bracelet. $295.00.

Memory wire red beaded necklace with earrings. Pendant drop and earrings have pavé rhinestones. $350.00.

Shaded white and blue glass beads of various sizes used in necklace and earrings. $175.00.

Creamy faux pearls, double strand necklace with blossom centerpiece that has diamente rhinestone center. Miniature blossoms emphasize clasp. $195.00.

Four strand necklace has frontal floral clasp with emerald cut crystal drop. Crystal earrings. $210.00.

Pearl bracelet and necklace. Notice Haskell clasps on both pieces. $140.00.

Single strand pearl necklace and earrings. Pendant has diamente rhinestones surrounding faux pearl. $155.00.

Lime green bead necklace and earrings. Antique gold with small green beads. $180.00.

Cranberry crystal bead necklace and earrings. $225.00.

Double strand pearl necklace with center medallion of pearls and diamente rhinestones. Note floral and clasp design. Earrings repeat the pearl and rhinestone motif. $295.00.

White and mint green carved beads, rhinestone rondels necklace, with matching mint green earrings. $175.00.

Patriotic necklace. Silver-plated with gold-plated national eagle symbol. $210.00.

Art Deco necklace of topaz and silver beads. $80.00

Six strand turquoise necklace, note clasp. $195.00.

Summer white chalk beads, long three strand necklace. $125.00.

Crystal bead necklace with silver turban spacers. $85.00.

Necklace with two strands of olive green crystal beads and middle row of 10 matching faceted stones in dog-tooth settings. $165.00.

Double strand pearl necklace, small clasp. $90.00.

Five strand pearl necklace with ornate pearl clasp. $220.00.

Top: Faux pearl brooch with gold leaves and small rhinestone and pearl flowers. Earrings. $150.00. Right: Long gold drop earrings incorporate gold balls and filigree décor. $165.00.

Gold-plated peacock brooch and earrings. Feathers outlined in strands of blue rhinestones. $350.00.

Top: Green cabochon is wrapped by rows of diamente rhinestones. $295.00. Bottom: Adjustable gold-plated, diamente studded ring. $125.00.

Top: Pink moonstone cabochon brooch with pink and clear rhinestones and pearls. $280.00. Right: Pink moonstone earrings with ten pink breads and three shaded pink drops. $145.00.

Left: Brooch with eight gold chain tassels that end in pink, blue, citrine, and topaz beads. Same beads encircle the brooch. $155.00. Right: Pearl and diamente rhinestone brooch. Gold chain ribbon bow with pearl tassels. $325.00.

Left: Lucite leaf brooch with pastel bead flowers uses small clear rhinestones for sparkle. $475.00. Right: Pearls of various sizes, gold leaves, small rhinestone brooch. $155.00.

Top: Summer chalk white beaded brooch. $110.00. Right: Summer chalk white beads sewn with strands of blue and red beads. $225.00.

Top: Brooch of three golden rings, topaz cabochons, and gold leaves. $95.00. Bottom: Gold-plated feather with golden filigree butterfly. $125.00.

Left: Antique gold stick pin, floral. $135.00. Right: Pearl stick pin with three pearl tassels. $175.00.

Parure of five strand bracelet, brooch, and earrings. Elaborate bracelet clasp repeats design on brooch and earrings. $395.00.

Left: Three pairs of earrings. Turquoise bead center with five diamente rhinestone points. $60.00. Middle: Light pink chalk beads form flower petal earrings. $45.00. Right: Silver-plated, topaz molded glass stones. $110.00.

Back of typical Haskell brooch showing the wiring and the stamped finding. The oval cartouche bears her name.

Left: Seed pearls rim diamente rhinestone earring center. Top: Matching comb ornament (original comb replaced) repeats the pearls, and pink rhinestones add accent. $300.00 set.

Pink bead multi-strand necklace has an overlay garland of the same beads in the soft pink shades. With earrings. $425.00 set.

Disciples of Haskell

Take the magic ingredients of seed pearls, antique gold leaves, brass wire, concave and convex findings, and needles, and you have the basis for a Haskell creation.

Haskell took her sewing abilities and created embroidery techniques of sewing the various items to a convex, stamped frame using brass so fine it resembled thread. All knots were carefully tied on the underneath side. When the dimensional design was finished, a concave or reverse stamped finding concealed all the knots. If a Haskell piece is closely examined, once again with that handy loupe, you will be able to see where the two pieces were tied together with that same brass thread.

Her jewelry creations were the inspiration for many designers. Some of them even served their novice years working for Haskell, developing their own skills, then going on into businesses of their own. Let's take a closer look at that jewelry.

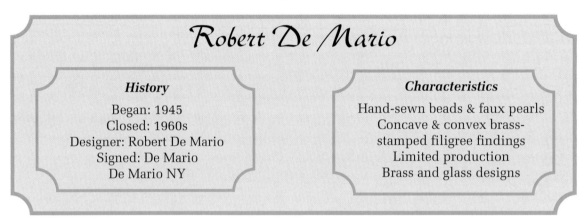

Robert De Mario

History
Began: 1945
Closed: 1960s
Designer: Robert De Mario
Signed: De Mario
De Mario NY

Characteristics
Hand-sewn beads & faux pearls
Concave & convex brass-stamped filigree findings
Limited production
Brass and glass designs

Miriam Haskell had a great influence in the world of costume jewelry in many ways. Under her tutelage many young designers tried their wings and developed their craft to a point where they left the nest to fly on their own.

One such young talent was Robert De Mario, free-lance designer in the early 1940s. He gained much experience working for many of the New York jewelry firms.

During that time he had the good fortune to make connections with the Miriam Haskell firm. In designing for her jewelry line, he quickly learned the techniques she had introduced, convex and concave brass-stamped filigree plate findings with layered hand-sewn beads, and pearls sewn with "thread" of fine brass wire.

The beads were strung with this brass thread and attached to the convex plate, then knotted underneath. This allowed multi-layers of pearls, beads, and leaves to be intertwined. All the knots were covered by the concave stamping when the two plates were wired together.

As World War II drew to an end, the nation returned to normalcy, and De Mario decided to set up his own jewelry business in New York City in 1945. Little did he know that the distinctive Haskell style of brass and glass would influence him the rest of his professional life. Some 15 years of De Mario's jewelry brought him his own recognition for workmanship and hands-on craftsmanship. The quality of all his jewelry earned him a well-deserved reputation for high standards.

Although his business was doing well, De Mario chose the time to close the doors forever and retired to Palm Beach, Florida. As you look through the following selection of pictures, you can see that he truly could rest on his laurels.

Three strand, aurora borealis beads. Longest strand is 16", shortest is 13". Note the DeMario flower that finishes off the small chain fastener. $195.00.

Nine strand golden double chain with random patterns of lemon and gray balls, faux pearls, faceted green beads. Matching 1¼" clip-back earrings. $90.00 – 115.00.

14" torsade of three small pearls strands, two strands of blue crystals. Ornate Haskell style clasp adds flowers with rhinestone centers, repeated in matching earrings. $265.00 – 330.00.

2½" crescent-shaped earrings, gold-plated, festooned with faux coral and turquoise beads, seed pearls, and diamente rhinestones. $95.00 – 110.00.

Top: Aquamarine molded glass petal brooch has dog-toothed prongs. $145.00. Bottom: 1½" gold-plated, clip-on earrings. Crystal beads, blue ball with pearls, gold flowers with rhinestone centers. $75.00.

Bracelet has two cross bars, four strands, ornate box clasp of pearl and rhinestone blossom. Matching four strands (longest is 20½") has same topaz faceted glass beads, faux pearls, and rhinestone rondels. $295.00.

19" double strand faux pearls with 1½" side accent design of marbleized cabochon petals with a pearl and rhinestone center. De Mario flower hook. $250.00.

Left: Green enamel and jade animal bracelet. $175.00. Right: Gold-plated, diamente pavé rhinestones. $115.00.

Four strand necklace, longest 17", peach and beige-colored pearls; amber glass beads, gold balls, and square nacre beads. $95.00.

Top: Brooch has aurora borealis beads and brass leaves. $180.00. Bottom left: Strung yellow beads, enamel white petals, yellow moonstone pearl earrings. $45.00. Bottom right: Brass flowers with rhinestone centers, gray pearl and white bead flower earrings. $80.00.

Five strand, gold-plated braid, tied in bow with four tassels ending in faux pearls. $475.00.

11" double strand teal blue crystal beads. Front fastener 1" center, 1¾" side pieces have gold leaves and gold beads also. $275.00.

3½" rigid centerpiece of fuchsia leaves, pearls, red and purple beads, aurora borealis rhinestone necklace suspended with twin 5" strands of pearls, faceted fuchsia, red, and purple beads. $350.00.

Brooch, 3" x 2½". Frosted pink tube bead flowers, overlay of pink rhinestones and gold leaves. $230.00.

12" choker necklace, 3 strands faux pearl, 1½" center design has seed pearl, diamente rhinestones, and gold leaves. $175.00.

Faux pearls, clear rhinestones, gold leaves brooch and matching earrings. $195.00.

Haskell look faux pearl parure choker necklace, six strand bracelet, and earrings. $450.00.

Chatelaine, double strand of blue and green beads with rhinestone rondels connecting the two brooches which use the same beads. $325.00.

Aquamarine parure (15" necklace, 6½" bracelet, and earrings). Faceted glass beads with brass spacers, faceted lentil beads capped with filigree diamente rhinestone studded petals. $875.00.

19" double strand necklace. Turban beads are mixed with faceted beads, both emerald green color, rhinestone rondels. 2" pendant of gold petaled blossoms, diamente and green rhinestones. $395.00.

Robert Originals, Inc.

History

Began: 1940s
Closed: 1984
Designers: Robert Levy
Larry Josephs
Ellen Jaffee Wagman

Characteristics

Artist palette used on cartouche
Haskell style of pearls and brass
Wonderful enameling

Another young designer who was greatly influenced by Haskell was Robert Levy. Many people mistakenly assume that Levy had at one time been an employee of Haskell because of his artistry in the use of pearls and brass.

Instead he chose another path. Joined by his friends Irving Landsman and David Jaffe, the three young men made their debut as Fashioncraft Jewelry Co., Inc. in New York City in the 1940s.

During that period the signature "Robert" was used. I have one piece marked with that printed downhill signature, the smiling figural at top left on page 90.

When Irving left the company after two years, David and Robert took Larry Josephs aboard. Larry stayed with the company nine years before he left to purchase the Hattie Carnegie jewelry business in 1957.

The remaining partners, Robert and David, decided to rename the company Robert Originals, Inc. The jewelry now displayed a trademark cartouche, an artist palette, proudly proclaiming "Original by Robert."

For the next 15 years the firm maintained a reputation that ensured their place in the theatrical world as a jewelry company who could provide Broadway with spectacular jewels.

Robert Levy retired in 1975, leaving David Jaffee, the remaining original partner, to run the business. He was not alone long, for daughter Ellen joined the company as president. She proved to be a skilled designer, and in 1979 the company was renamed Ellen Designs for Robert Originals.

The year 1984 marked the firm's becoming Ellen Designs. Ellen Jaffee Wagman and John Wagman, her husband, continued the tradition so firmly established by her father and Robert. Her jewelry is marked with the artist palette and Ellen Designs, and this brings our story up-to-date.

Imitation jade and pearl parure of necklace, bracelet, and earrings. The look of Haskell. $245.00.

Gold turban beads with brown balls, parure of necklace, brooch, and earrings. Brooch and earrings also have brown and gold rhinestones. $180.00.

"Haskell" faux pearl parure of bracelet, necklace, and earrings. $275.00.

Left: Gold-plated necklace with gold and silver coated rhinestones. $110.00. Right: Red and aurora borealis rhinestone earrings. $52.00.

Faux pearls and diamente rhinestone necklace and earrings. Blue rhinestone accents. $175.00.

Triple strand faux pearl necklace and brooch. Gold leaves and diamente rhinestones. $200.00.

Triple strand beads have typical Haskell style clasp. $165.00.

Five strand necklace with large amethyst crystal in clasp. Beads are pink, lavender, and purple. $325.00.

Left: Pink crystals and dusty rose rhinestone star. $105.00. Right and bottom: Blue and pink crystals, blue rhinestone sword and earrings. $295.00 set.

Left: Faux pearl, diamente rhinestone brooch and earrings. $180.00. Right: Faux pearl and diamente brooch and earrings. $165.00.

Pink pearls, clear and pink rhinestone brooch and earrings. $195.00.

Fashioncraft smiling figural. Silver with remarkable detail, 1½" tall. Blue, red, and green enameled shirt decoration with 13 multicolored dangles on hat. $350.00.

Crescent moon made in two pieces wired together has mobile of aquamarine crystals and silver leaves, adorned with pearls and blue rhinestones. $450.00.

Diamente rhinestone brooch. $145.00.

Haskell look faux pearl brooch. $130.00.

Brooch of pink beads tipped with clear rhinestones, rhinestone and gold ribbon accent. $105.00.

Left: Gold twist brooch with green rhinestones and faux pearls. $98.00. Right: Faux pearl earrings rimmed with crystal and rhinestone rondels. $65.00.

Left: Gold-plated nosegay brooch with white enamel flowers. Centers are clear rhinestones. $80.00. Right: Emerald green rhinestone brooch. $80.00.

Ruby crystal is emerald cut, framed with purple rhinestones and outlined in red beads. $350.00.

Star brooch with pink glass centerpiece. Pink rhinestones and seed pearls. $185.00.

Left: Black and white enamel flower. $78.00. Right: Red enamel flower, black stamen and pistils. $65.00.

Left: Yellow enamel blossom has black bee feeding on white pollen center. $98.00. Right: White enamel flower edged in black has red ladybug. $98.00.

Top: Yellow and brown enamel butterfly. $54.00. Bottom left: Enamel fruit. $45.00. Bottom right: Pink enamel flower. $55.00.

Pot-belly stove. $70.00.

Top: Red enamel strawberry. $45.00. Bottom left: Black enamel mushroom. $55.00. Bottom right: Red enamel apple. $60.00.

Enamel Christmas tree with red bead ornaments. $110.00.

Proud white enamel rooster. $90.00.

Top: Enamel dragonfly. $78.00. Bottom: Enamel red cardinal. $65.00

Enamel shoulder grasshopper. $145.00.

Top: Enamel land turtle. $75.00. Bottom: Enamel ocean turtle. $80.00.

Faux pearl earrings with pink and blue rhinestones, blue and gold bead drops. $90.00

Left: Faux pearl and red blossom brooch. $135.00. Right: Double strand red bead necklace. $110.00.

The Hollywood silver screen brought glamor to the most rural corner of the United States. Theater goers fell in love with the beautiful stars in glorious costumes who were larger than life. They went home and dreamed of the jewelry and fine gowns they had seen. And those dreams became part of their reality by buying costume jewelry made by the following designers.

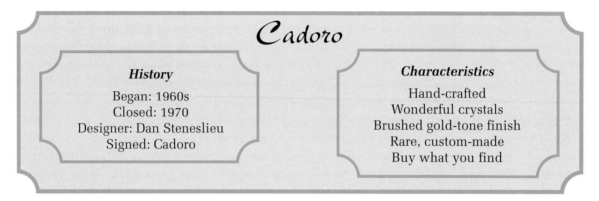

Cadoro

History

Began: 1960s
Closed: 1970
Designer: Dan Steneslieu
Signed: Cadoro

Characteristics

Hand-crafted
Wonderful crystals
Brushed gold-tone finish
Rare, custom-made
Buy what you find

The glamor of Hollywood was personified by Steven Brody, a 1950s movie star. His leading man roles earned him a ranking in the international jet set and afforded him an open invitation to European social events.

There he met Dan Steneslieu, a descendant of the Romanian royal family. The two young world travelers shared a passion for beautiful artwork.

They formed the firm of Cadoro, incorporating the old world designs of Russia and Romania, combining their common loves for art and travel, collecting antique jewelry stones and fittings from all over Europe. It may have been considered just a lark when the two young men started their own jewelry line, but Cadoro soon became a respected name in the jewelry world.

Each piece was a hand-crafted custom design, truly fashion trend-setters prized by the jet set. They utilized brushed gold-tone metal finishes almost as a trademark. The golden Christmas tree (bottom of page 95) is still gleaming, each and every branch, after all these years. Can you find all nine partridges whose spreading wings form the branches and the green pear that dangles from the lowest branch?

The breathtaking crystals these men found in Europe were of gorgeous shades. The 1¾" square brooch (at top right on page 95) has just four crystals, but they are magnificent, faceted emerald cut ones. Apricot, the color of sunkissed peaches, enhances the shade of blue that is the color of the spring sky.

Cadoro had an unlimited supply of wonderful cabochons also and used them to full advantage.

Many times they would use dog-toothed prongs, so named because the many prongs encircled the stones like a set of dog's teeth, to firmly grasp the stones.

To me, the spirit of these two men who were world travelers, adventurers, romantics, and artists has flown into the sea creature seen in at top left on page 95, brought to life from the ocean's depth by the warmth of the brightly colored red and green cabochons nestled in the golden body and enhanced by the blue lapis stones that are his scales — I call it an Art Nouveau masterpiece.

When Dan tragically died in the 1960s, the loss of his friend and of Dan's designing talent was a double-strength blow that Steven could not handle. The firm was closed down in 1970.

Death was too real, and the story does not have a happy ending.

One-inch diameter green jasper cabochon brooch. $90.00.

Left: Gold blossom, center red cabochon framed with seed pearls. $95.00. Right: Sea creature. $450.00.

Four crystal square brooch. $220.00.

One-inch diameter imitation onyx brooch. $90.00.

Sapphire blue cabochon, four trios of pearls, pavé diamente rhinestones. $210.00.

A cascade of imitation amber beads carried by three golden doves. $185.00.

Gold and silver leaves, small rhinestone bug. $195.00.

Golden Christmas tree. $225.00.

Hobé

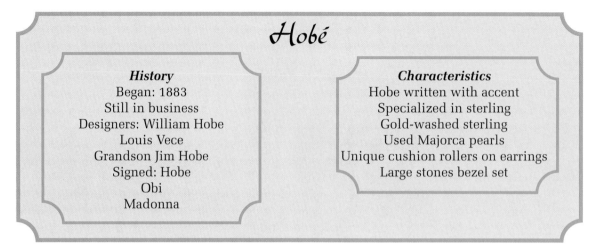

History
Began: 1883
Still in business
Designers: William Hobe
Louis Vece
Grandson Jim Hobe
Signed: Hobe
Obi
Madonna

Characteristics
Hobe written with accent
Specialized in sterling
Gold-washed sterling
Used Majorca pearls
Unique cushion rollers on earrings
Large stones bezel set

For four generations the inheritance of each Hobé son had been the great name of Hobé and all the jewelry knowledge that has been acquired since patriarch Jacques Hobé created his first masterpiece. He was a Parisian master craftsman offering jewelry which had earned him such a high reputation that he became royal jeweler to the court of France. He introduced the newest methods of mass production to make jewelry befitting the king.

Son William served as his apprentice to learn the trade secrets until the interruption of the guns of war when William saw service as a soldier for France during World War II.

Recovering from his wartime experience, William moved to sunny California, but his hands did not stay idle for long. He soon was designing buckles, and by 1920 he had moved to New York and opened the doors of the Hobé Button Company. With a great love for his mother country, William interpreted historical designs with modern settings and offered a small collection to the public. Wife Sylvia Kittner was both working partner and stylist.

The company specialized in sterling or gold-washed sterling set with semi-precious stones in both antique reproductions and new designs. With tremendous standards of excellence, Hobé was able to offer and affirm "quality not neglected in affordable pieces of jewelry."

The high standards were entrusted to William and Sylvia's sons, Robert and Donald, as their inheritance. The company catered to the Hollywood stars who would wear the jewelry that looked like the real thing but without the expensive price tag.

Glamorous Carole Lombard, Bette David, Barbara Stanwyck, Mae West, and Mary Martin were among the stars who wore Hobé on stage and off.

In the 1930s, Hobe made complete jewelry wardrobes for director Cecil B. DeMille. Edith Head drew on these historical pieces to enhance her studio fashion designs used in the movie industry.

Every 20 years the company changed its logo, and it has recorded six changes in the almost 120 years that have well established the Hobé tradition: crossed sword logo was used 1883 to 1902; Hobé written with an accent in oval cartouche, 1903 – 1917; house-shaped outline has first line Hobé, second line Design Pat, 1918 – 1932; triangle outline, first line Hobé, second line Design Pat., 1933 – 1957; Hobé written with accent and copyright © in oval, 1958 – 1963; Hobé with accent, 1999; and current mark is Hobé with an accent, the copyright © placed over the o.

Wouldn't it be lovely if all jewelry companies had kept such wonderful recorded histories?

"Carmen Miranda"-style parure of necklace, bracelet, and earrings. Shaded yellow and pink beads combined with chalk white ones has green glass leaves and plastic tropical fruit. $225.00.

96

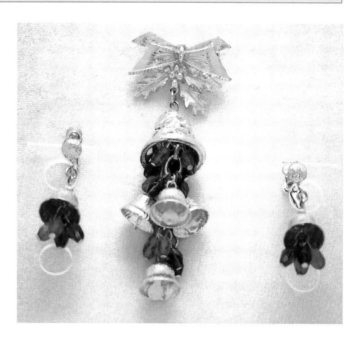

Christmas necklace and bracelet of golden bells with red and green bead pairs between. Part of grand parure priced at right.

Brooch and earrings complete a grand parure when combined with the necklace and bracelet at left. Full parure of necklace, bracelet, brooch, and earrings, $750.00.

Left: Earrings and necklace set. Gold chain with pendant of ruby, sapphire, and diamente rhinestones. Repeated design in earrings. $175.00 set. Right: Five alternating rows on necklace of red rhinestones, diamente rhinestones, red rhinestones, gold chain, red rhinestones. Earrings have rows of diamente, red, and diamente rhinestones around central blue crystal. $240.00 set.

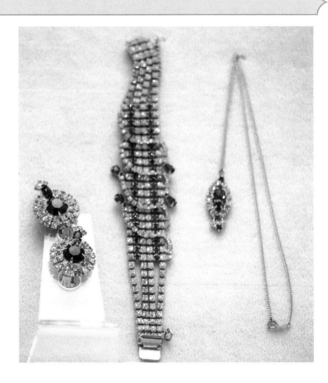

Peking glass bead parure necklace, bracelet, and earrings feature Venetian gold foil glass beads. Twisted gold chain is used between each bead strand. $375.00 set.

Emerald green rhinestones featured in parure of earrings, bracelet, and necklace. Diamente rhinestones give sparkling radiance. $250.00 set.

Silver-plated parure with diamente rhinestones bracelet, necklace, and earrings. $210.00 set.

Summer pink and blue pear-shaped rhinestone parure. The inner row of the necklace and both outside bracelet rows have faux pearls. Earrings have a pearl in the center. $295.00 set.

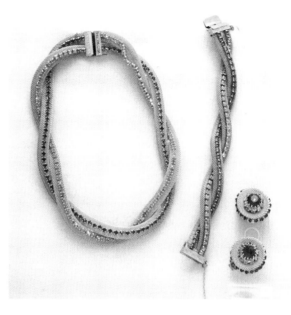

Gold mesh parure of necklace, bracelet, and earrings. Topaz rhinestones. $195.00 set.

Green and blue bead earrings, bracelet, and necklace. $300.00 set.

Frosted bead necklace, bracelet, and earrings parure. Citrine and green rhinestones. $210.00 set.

Frosted white bead and diamente rondel parure necklace, spring wire bracelet, and earrings. $250.00 set.

Gold flowers with rhinestone centers, linked with olive green crystal and gold beads. Parure of bracelet, necklace, and earrings. $275.00 set.

Summer white chalk molded glass novelty beads with gold veined bead centers. Parure necklace, cuff bracelet, and earrings. $210.00 set.

Gold parure necklace, mesh bracelet, and earrings. Necklace is French garland style with diamente rhinestones of various sizes. $295.00 set.

Gold chain strings three strands of faux pearl and turquoise beads with gold caps. Spring wire bracelet and earrings. $150.00 set.

Gold chain strings white chalk beads with sections of clear rondels and red beads in parure necklace, bracelet, and earrings. Spring wire wrap bracelet. $135.00 set.

Triple strand red parure necklace, bracelet, and earrings with gold-plated bars. Plastic beads. $135.00 set.

Diamente rhinestone and frosted crystal necklace and earrings. $195.00.

Left: Locket hangs on double gold chain, has topaz, green, and diamente rhinestones. Pattern repeats on earrings. $225.00. Right: Blue crystal double strand necklace and earrings. $125.00.

Left: Black and white bead necklace and earrings. $95.00. Right: Gold-plated necklace has chain with pendant of diamente baguettes and chatons with small pearls. Matching earrings. $210.00.

Left: Chartreuse square rhinestone necklace and earrings. $90.00. Right: Triple strand necklace of crystal, gold, and champagne beads. $70.00.

Left and bottom: Pink frosted beads, rhinestone rondels used in double strand necklace with large gold-plated center medallion. Matching spring wire triple row bracelet. $25.00. Right: Frosted pink and clear navettes triple strand necklace. One matching earring. $75.00.

Left: Chalk white earrings and matching necklace. Blue rhinestones used for color. $135.00. Right: Chalk white beads, pearls, and crackle black novelty glass stones earrings and necklace. $110.00

Left: Ceramic center stone with painted yellow and brown modernistic butterfly necklace. Yellow and brown woven cord chain. $150.00. Right: Blue and clear four strand beaded necklace. $85.00.

Top: Charm bracelet with caged pearls dangle. $45.00. Bottom: Pink and blue cuff bracelet. $45.00. Right: Pink beads, white popcorn beads bracelet and necklace. $54.00.

Left: Earrings and bracelet combine pearls and diamente rhinestones. $78.00. Middle: Earrings and mesh bracelet feature chalk white navettes with orange rhinestones. $105.00. Right: Citrine crystal bead earrings and spring wire bracelet. $75.00.

Left: 50-year-old gold and silver twisted chain choker. $100.00. Right: Carved, wooden bead necklace. $40.00.

Egyptian influence, golden interlocking rings necklace. $275.00.

Left: Chalk white and lavender beads, five strand necklace. $40.00. Right: Topaz bead necklace with molded glass petaled flower. $98.00.

Hammered gold chain, locket has light and dark rhinestones. $195.00.

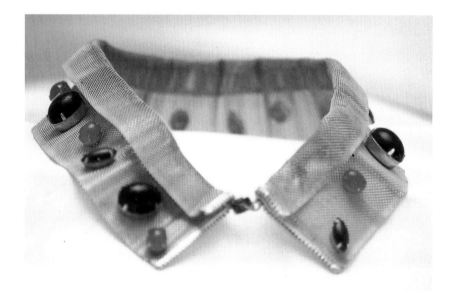

Zippered mesh collar with imitation stones. $225.00.

Left: Alternating rhinestone rows of diamente and blue rinestone brooch and earrings. $110.00. Right: Gold-plated single stem flower with flower bud earrings. Pavé, diamente inner petals, and pearl centers. $145.00.

Top: Two renderings of the same design brooch, one done in black rhinestones, $95.00; another in emerald green and diamente rhinestones, $120.00. Bottom: Enamel earrings and brooch. Flower has pink rhinestone center. $60.00.

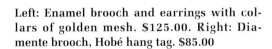

Left: Enamel brooch and earrings with collars of golden mesh. $125.00. Right: Diamente brooch, Hobé hang tag. $85.00

Left: Topaz and Hershey brown rhinestones with pavé crescents, brooch and earrings. $165.00. Right: Gold-plated emerald green rhinestone centers rimmed with seed pearls. Clear rhinestone leaves, brooch and earrings. $175.00.

Left and top: Empress Eugene dress clip and earrings, multicolored rhinestones. $450.00. Right: Enamel leaves, lavender and amethyst grape earrings and brooch. $275.00.

Left top and bottom: Aurora borealis, blue rhinestone, three-dimensional, diamente rhinestone petals. Brooch and earrings. $195.00. Middle: Pink rhinestone spray ribbon of pavé diamente rhinestones. Brooch and earrings. $135.00. Right: White porcelain rose brooch and earrings. Hand-painted gold touches. $225.00.

Sterling silver, pink vermeil brooch and earrings. Pastel yellow, pink, green, and lavender crystals. $395.00.

Top left: Sterling silver brooch. $195.00. Top right: Sterling silver bow and roses brooch. $390.00. Bottom: Sterling silver bow. $410.00.

Top: Sterling silver bow, lavender crystal in center of flower. $425.00. Bottom: Pink vermeil sterling silver bow. $495.00.

Left: Vermeil sterling silver, aquamarine crystal bow and earrings. $550.00.
Right: Vermeil sterling silver, topaz crystal brooch and earrings. $495.00.

Left: Yellow seed beads, small gray rhinestones brooch and earrings. $54.00. Right: Antique gold-plated, green crystals, and pearls brooch/earrings. $85.00.

Left: Dress clip and matching earrings. Pink and blue crystals. $395.00. Right: Sterling silver flowers. $125.00.

Top: Silver spray brooch. $250.00. Bottom: Pearl and diamente rhinestone brooch. $80.00.

Top left: Green, brown, lemon, and clear rhinestone brooch. $70.00. Top right: Imitation jade, gold leaves, clear rhinestone brooch. $45.00. Bottom: Yellow and blue rhinestones, gold-veined white cabochons. $90.00.

Top left: Strawberry, enamel leaves, red and clear rhinestones. $65.00. Top right: Matte gold-plated brooch, seed pearls and clear rhinestones. $40.00. Bottom: Mother-of-pearl petals, pearl center rimmed with clear rhinestones brooch. $72.00.

Top: White enamel, multicolored cabochons. $30.00. Middle left: Large blue cabochons, matching blue rhinestone, clear rhinestone frame. $78.00. Middle right: Aurora borealis circle brooch. $60.00. Bottom: Shaded blue rhinestones, pavé diamente petals flower bud brooch. $85.00.

Left: Imitation jade cabochon bracelet. $65.00. Right: Imitation jade cabochon bracelet, gold-plated leaves. $65.00.

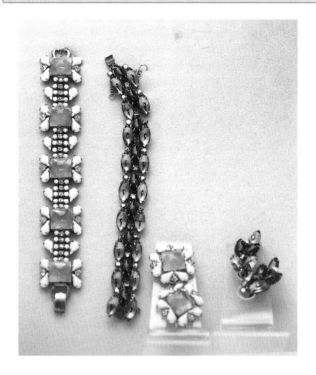

Left: White navettes, pink treated square cabochon bracelet and earrings. $68.00. Right: Tri-color navettes are yellow, blue, and green in bracelet and matching earrings. $80.00.

Left: Sterling silver rose link bracelet. $175.00. Middle: Sterling silver flower link bracelet. $225.00. Right: Sterling silver link bracelet and earrings. Aquamarine crystals. $350.00.

Lavender bracelet, 1960s hand-faceted 1" dentelle with small lavender rhinestones. Matching hoop earrings cover entire ear. $480.00.

Collection of earrings ranging from $48.00 to $95.00.

Top left: Imitation opal wings, faux ruby cabochon body butterfly. $95.00. Top right: Gold-plated Christmas wreath with green rhinestones. Red rhinestone candle with a diamente flame. $130.00. Center left: Silver donkey. $50.00. Center right: Art Deco silver and gold owl. $45.00. Bottom: Gold and clear rhinestone cat. Brown cabochon body with brown rhinestone ears. $75.00.

Left: Gold-plated alligator with red rhinestones. $50.00. Middle top: Gold rhinestone chicken peeks out of green rhinestone egg. $155.00. Middle bottom: Golden monkey has motion eyes. $60.00. Right: Blue-eyed animal. $35.00.

111

Processed ivory Oriental maiden. $300.00.

Red, white, and blue glass stones, white enameled clown. $225.00.

Top: Golden leopard, green rhinestone eyes. $140.00. Bottom left: Gold-plated rabbit. $80.00. Bottom right: Lamb, gold bell collar, rat tail forelocks, green rhinestone eyes. $150.00.

Chatelaine, imitation jade stones. $210.00.

Hobé hang tag. Earrings have been positioned to show cushion roller.

Joseff of Hollywood

History

Began: 1935
Still in business
Designer: Eugene Joseff
Signed: Joseff – 1938
Joseff of Hollywood
1930s – 1940s

Characteristics

Special antique gold and silver finish
Hand-soldered
Hand-set
Originals rented to movies
Copies were retailed

Eugene Joseff was born in Chicago, but he owed Hollywood for his rise to stardom. How an advertising professional evolved into the "Jeweler for the Silver Screen" would make a blockbuster movie.

The film would begin by showing Joseff puttering around in his free time, experimenting with jewelry designs for almost two years. An evening spent going to the movies proved to be the turning point. Sitting in the darkened theater watching a historical movie, during a tender love scene he roared with laughter at the heroine. She was dressed in period costume but had on jewels from her contemporary jewelry box. He had found his niche. He would create historically correct jewelry for movie studios.

Then came his first sale, one bracelet and four buttons. It took two years for that first step, but by 1937 he had movie studios clamoring for his work. He would spend hours, even days, researching material to make sure that he was creating the right jewelry for the time period covered in the script.

Because of the camera lights he invented a special formula for antique gold and silver plating to prevent glare. The finest rhinestones were imported from Czechoslovakia and Austria, and highly skilled employees used every possible material from precious stones, gold, silver to wood, glass, tin, and plastic to bring his designs to life. Even ebony and ivory were duplicated by injection-molded acetate processes. The pieces were cast and stamped from brass, hand-soldered and hand-set in the same method applied to precious metals and real jewelry.

Drawing on his first profession, advertising, his contract with the studios outlined a rental process. Yes, you could see that beautiful necklace was adorning the star of the movie, but it was only leased and really belonged to Joseff. The pieces became the backbone for the Joseff retail line in 1937.

Only one boutique per major city was allowed to carry the jewelry produced for the public. The original design was never sold to the public. From the late 1930s to the late 1950s, 90 percent of Hollywood jewelry was produced by Joseff.

Straight from the camera lights when the movie was completed, the jewelry left the wardrobe department and went into the rental library that housed over 3,000,000 pieces — a true treasure house of costume jewelry.

Television shows such as "Dynasty," "Murder, She Wrote," and "Mission Impossible" have library cards for this unique archive now owned by Mrs. Joan Castle Joseff. Although Joseff died in 1948, his widow has successfully continued his line, keeping his name and star shining brightly.

Sun God with dangling rhinestone eyes and earrings. $325.00.

Antique gold-plated flower. $225.00.

Blue plastic flower petals, gold center. $200.00.

Left: Silver filigree, blue marquise rhinestone, and diamente rhinestone brooch. $250.00. Right: Four topaz stones and gold brooch. $300.00.

Large center dentelle, eight small gold flowers, light blue rhinestone brooch. $650.00.

Amethyst and filigree cross necklace. $750.00.

Gold-plated bearded man wearing turban. $280.00.

Left: Frog sitting on leaf. $375.00. Right: Antique gold-plated bee. $175.00.

Antique gold, matte finish bow. $450.00.

Silver plated, three sizes of owls' heads necklace. $295.00.

Silver bracelet, fuchsia glass stones, leaf clasp. $280.00.

Gold flower bracelet and earrings. $235.00.

There were many companies that were capable of doing all the stages of jewelry production. From designing to model making, from casting to plating, everything was done within the confines of some companies.

And many of the manufacturers were also responsible for doing work on behalf of other companies, taking the designs brought to them and making them a reality. All of the production done for another company was always marked by the manufacturer with the client's company name.

Sometimes the pieces were left without any marks and were wholesaled to various companies such as J.C. Penney or Sears & Roebuck, or sold to fine jewelry stores to be placed in the store's presentation boxes, carded or assigned a hang tag.

The following four companies represent this special segment of the jewelry industry: Ralph De Rosa, Florenza, Hollycraft, and Weiss.

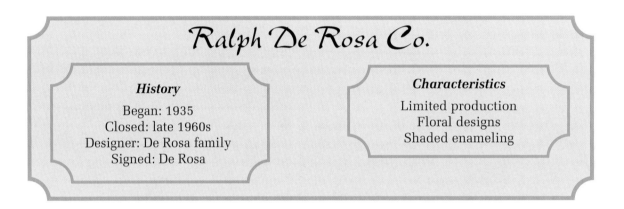

Ralph De Rosa Co.

History

Began: 1935
Closed: late 1960s
Designer: De Rosa family
Signed: De Rosa

Characteristics

Limited production
Floral designs
Shaded enameling

The Ralph De Rosa Company was located at 404 Fourth Avenue in New York City. You could find their doors open from 1935 to the latter part of 1960s.

If you had the great fortune to visit their company, you would find there not only Ralph but three other members of the De Rosa family, Elvira, Virginia, and Theresa. The company was truly family operated.

They were a jewelry manufacturer, spending most of their time putting other people's names on their production. One of their major clients was Elsa Schiaparelli. They used their excellent craftsmanship to execute Schiaparelli's designs, producing jewelry fashions to complete her costumes.

De Rosa found little time to create their own designs and market them with the De Rosa trademark. Because of the labor intensive designs they made, these were done in limited production, making De Rosa pieces rare and hard to find.

Look for floral designs accented by exquisite shaded enameling. A few examples of their design work follow; please study them so you can find more of these hidden treasures.

2½" brooch with glass blue and red stones and gold pear-shaped rhinestones. $325.00.

1½" Art Nouveau earrings. Gold-plated, scattered diamente rhinestones. Pink cabochon flowers with clear rhinestone centers. $180.00.

3" imitation diamond rhinestone brooch in Art Deco six-pointed shape. $275.00.

Faux turquoise cabochons embedded in antique gold-plated circle brooch. $225.00.

Gold-plated fur clip with emerald green cabochons. $350.00.

Fur clip with five white enamel bells with red bead clappers. Red enamel bow and pavé diamente rhinestone stars. $395.00.

Gold-plated crown brooch with four faux pearls and green and orange rhinestones. $425.00.

Florenza

History

Began: 1948
Closed: 1981
Designer: Daniel Kasoff
Signed: Florenza

Characteristics

Antique gold finish
Old World look
Novelty glass stones
Pieces' backs always finished

Designer Daniel Kasoff worked hard to achieve his professional standing. Born Dave Kosovsky, this first-generation New Yorker had a short childhood. He took on the role of a man while still in short pants when he took on the role of bread winner for his widowed mother and five sisters.

He worked hard in the garment industry to bring home food and keep a roof over their heads. A misfortune and a kindness enabled him to make contact with the owner of Speier Costume Jewelry.

Young Dan had his coat stolen in a restaurant. Mr. Speier, who was dining in the restaurant, saw his distress and came to his rescue with enough money to get another coat.

As soon as he could, Dan went to repay Mr. Speier and was rewarded for his honesty with a job at the jewelry company, just the start he needed. Dan stayed with the company for 10 years, learning the business from the ground up.

By 1948 he was able to open the doors of his own business, the Dan Kasoff Company. The next eight years saw a tremendous growth in his business. He was selling his products to wholesalers worldwide, and his pieces could be found in department stores and specialty shops.

In 1950, Kasoff welcomed his son, Larry, into the company. The two men decided to protect their designs and registered their line. They took the name Florenza, named after Dan's wife, Florence. Much of the jewelry had a distinctive Old World look, featuring antique goldtone metal, stone, and settings to simulate fine antique jewelry.

Kasoff's wholesale customers included Weiss, Kramer, Coro, Capri, Carnegie, and Revlon. They would bring instructions, and the Kasoff design department would interpret their instructions into pictorial renditions for the client's approval. Then the factory division would get involved, and the finished product would bear the name of the customer.

All designs were the property of those customers.

Only Kasoff original creations were marked Florenza, with destinations such as Saks Fifth Avenue, Bloomingdale's, and Lord and Taylor. Hollycraft, BSK, Art, and Florenza were four companies in the manufacturing circle in the 1940s.

Sadly the company closed its doors for medical reasons in 1980. Although no longer producing jewelry, Larry is still in love with jewelry.

Parure of necklace, bracelet, and earrings. Specialty glass cabochons of iridescent pink to blue with aurora borealis rhinestones. $180.00.

Gold-plated necklace and earrings. Faux pearls, bronze rhinestones, with diamente aurora borealis rhinestones. $115.00.

A set of gold-plated necklace with two versions of earrings. Faceted watermelon glass stones are accented by aurora borealis rhinestones. $150.00 set.

Left: Earrings and matching necklace have gray faceted glass stones. Accents of gold and diamente rhinestones. $105.00.
Right: Enameled brooch and earrings. Pearl and lavender enamel beads. $250.00 set.

Left: Summer white necklace, one row of diamente rhinestones. $78.00. Middle and right: Black and white necklace and earrings. White milk glass stones and black rhinestones. $110.00.

Maltese cross with amethyst crystals, silver-plated. $175.00.

Faux pearl necklace and bracelet. Trimmed with crescents of pearls and diamente rhinestones. Four strand adjustable lariat necklace. Five strand bracelet with pearl and rhinestone clasp. $300.00.

Back of the lariat necklace at left, showing how the crescent opens to allow strands to be adjusted.

Left: Gold-plated twisted braid chain necklace with large medallion. $65.00. Right: Florentine necklace, gold-plated double strand. Faux pearls, green and lavender rhinestones. $90.00.

Left: Gold-plated chain pendant necklace. Open work design with four blue and one green cabochon. $55.00. Right: Paisley feather brooch. Blue cabochons, aurora borealis rhinestones. Center rib of diamente rhinestones. $105.00.

Matching necklace and bracelet. Frosted glass navettes, aurora borealis and citrine rhinestones. $150.00.

Bottom row: Three pairs of earrings matching brooches above. Values include earrings. Top: Basketweave brooch, gold-plated, multicolored rhinestones and earrings. $75.00. Left center: Maltese cross features four tulip glass stones, imitation pearl and turquoise stones. Blue center glass stone. Right center: Maltese cross, intaglio carved center stone. $195.00.

Left: Twin flowers with shades of pink and blue rhinestones, brooch and earrings. $145.00. Right: Maltese cross with multicolored pastel rhinestones. With matching earrings. $110.00.

Left: Brooch and earrings. Large emerald cut, citrine crystal centers, small seed pearls, topaz rhinestones. $140.00. Right: Brooch and earrings have crackled iridescent cabochons, curved seed pearls, square Peking glass stones. $200.00.

Left: Starfish brooch and earrings. Pink and purple rhinestones. $180.00. Right: Maltese cross in shades of blue rhinestones with cabochons. Matching earrings. $180.00.

Top: Antique design brooch with opalene cabochons, ruby red rhinestones. $225.00. Bottom: Sweater guard matches brooch with s-shaped cabochons at left. $80.00.

Left: Gold-plated star brooch with large faux turquoise bead, seed pearls, and topaz rhinestones. $55.00. Center top and bottom: Amber ribbed glass centers, enameled leaves, black and topaz rhinestones. Brooch and earrings. $275.00. Right: S-shaped cabochons, aurora borealis rhinestones, and seed pearls brooch. $110.00.

Top: Starfish brooch in lavender and purple rhinestones. $85.00. Bottom left: White seed pearl cluster tipped in topaz rhinestones, topaz cabochon center. $110.00. Bottom right: Japanned finish, black rhinestone brooch. $65.00.

Top: Glass flower stones topped with aurora borealis rhinestones, has small pearls. $45.00. Bottom left: Basketweave brooch with sapphire blue baguettes. $80.00. Bottom right: Aurora borealis tulips and rhinestones. $95.00.

123

Top: Pinwheel brooch with lavender glass center, four cats-eye cabochons, and shaded glass tones. $135.00. Left: Three turban glass stones, silver-frosted imitation onyx, and curved faux pearls flower brooch. $140.00. Right: Faux turquoise center and beads, pearls. Points are blue rhinestones. $95.00.

Left: Earrings and matching bracelet feature diamente and green rhinestones in a flowers and leaf pattern. $80.00. Right: Earrings and matching bracelet with shades of green rhinestones. $95.00.

Left: Bracelet of large lavender faceted glass stones with seed pearls in five repeated patterns. $55.00. Right: Summer white enamel bracelet and earrings. Touches of pastel rhinestones. $90.00.

Left: Bracelet and matching earrings. Blue cabochons and aurora borealis rhinestones. $80.00. Right: Matching earrings and bracelet, gold rhinestones, olive green faceted glass center stones, and small pearls. $90.00.

Left: Gold-plated link bracelet with multicolored rhinestones. $35.00. Right: Acorn bracelet with leaves. $60.00. Bottom: Bracelet with aurora borealis rhinestones and leaves. $40.00.

Top: Gold-plated bird's nest on branch has three pearl eggs, blue enamel bird. $75.00. Left: Pearl bug, crackle glass wings. $50.00. Right: Turquoise bead wings, faux pearl body insect, diamente rhinestone head. $45.00.

Left: Winged costumed man, enameled. $68.00. Right: White enamel, circus horse with blue enamel trim. Blue rhinestone eye. $95.00.

Left: Trembler brooch with earrings. Blue and aurora borealis rhinestones. $150.00. Right: Gold-plated, enamel owl with crackle glass belly. $80.00.

Top: Spotted leopard, gold-plated, enamel dots, green rhinestone eyes. $85.00. Bottom, left: Black cat, red rhinestone "13" on diamente rhinestone collar. $90.00. Bottom right: Gold-plated lion statue. $50.00.

Left: White enamel nodding poodle, purple pin cushion on back. $75.00. Right: Dancing poodle, enameled skirt and bonnet, diamente rhinestone accents. $45.00.

126

Left: Gold-plated hobo, faceted emerald green crystal head and poke. Multicolored rhinestone patches. $75.00. Right: Winged cherub, faux pearls, rhinestone eyes. $90.00.

Top: Gold-plated owl, black enamel feathers, pavé diamente rhinestones around enamel eye. $35.00. Bottom left: White enamel owl with plastic black beaded eyes that roll. $95.00. Bottom right: Gold-plated swan, black enamel wings, diamente rhinestone body. $40.00.

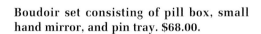

Boudoir set consisting of pill box, small hand mirror, and pin tray. $68.00.

Hollycraft Jewelry Company

History

Began: 1948
Closed: 1972
Designer: Joseph Chorbagian
Signed: Hollycraft 1948 – 1950
Hollycraft Corp with year
1950 – 1958

Characteristics

Year of production indicated
from
1950 through 1958
Whimsical/novelty items
usually are not dated
Distinctive pastel rhinestones

Seventeen-year-old Joseph Chorbagian left his home in Marash, Turkey, in 1917 to find his fortune in the United States. The streets were not lined with gold, but he accepted the challenge of making his own way in the country he had adopted.

Cousin Archie and a friend Jack Hazard pooled their resources with Joseph. They formed the Hollycraft Jewelry Company in 1948. The trio opened at 902 Broadway in New York City.

Their Victorian designs were sold to jobbers who produced the pieces in antique gold finish that usually served as backgrounds for their distinctive pastel rhinestones in unsurpassed shadings of blue, green, lavender, pink, and yellow.

During the first two years in business, their jewelry was marked Hollycraft. Most of their whimsical and novelty line of jewelry from seasonal Christmas to fresh fruit motifs falls into this category.

Much to the delight of today's collectors, in 1950 the company began marking their pieces with the year of manufacture. When the pieces are grouped by year, it is easy to compare the color variations.

In 1950 pastels were softer, more delicate shades. Seed pearls were the theme for 1950, and cat-eye cabochons glowed in the 1958 brooches.

The company discontinued business in the 1960s. It was sold in 1972 and closed its doors forever a short time later.

Cat-eye glass cabochon parure of earrings, brooch, and necklace. Soft green with aurora borealis rhinestones. $340.00.

Pastel green parure of bracelet, necklace, and earrings. Aurora borealis rhinestones. $295.00.

Floral pattern and chain fastener are typical of this company. Pastel green parure of earrings, necklace, and brooch. Please note the decorative finishing chain of necklace. $320.00.

Gold-plated, red rhinestone parure. Necklace, brooch, and earrings. $340.00.

Top: Pastel rhinestone leaf brooch. Earrings on bottom left. $125.00. Bottom: Circular brooch, large lavender rhinestone center stone, earrings to the right. $145.00.

Parure of bracelet, necklace, and earrings, pastel rhinestones. $190.00.

Right: Entwined gold-plated heart, blue rhinestone brooch. Left: Imitation jade, pearls, green and red rhinestones brooch with earrings. $80.00.

Three pairs of earrings. $35.00 – $50.00 pair. Front: Three rings. $40.00 – $50.00.

Diamente brooch and earrings. $95.00.

Top: Bow, pearl, and diamente rosettes. $65.00. Middle: Bow trimmed in blue. $80.00. Bottom: Silver bow, faux turquoise stones and blue rhinestones. Matching earrings. $110.00.

Root beer glass, clear rhinestone necklace and earrings. $80.00.

Left: Faux turquoise and blue rhinestone brooch. $70.00. Right: Enamel brooch and earrings, red rhinestones. $65.00.

Left: Red and green rhinestones, novelty candle tree with trunk in stand, earrings have dimpled gold ball at top. $150.00. Middle: Tree has clear stone trunk, earrings at bottom right have single, central candle. Multicolored rhinestones. $150.00. Right: Red-potted holly tree with red rhinestone berries and pearls. $85.00.

Top: Garland tree and earrings, bottom left: Multicolored rhinestones. $135.00. Bottom: Multicolored rhinestone tree and earrings. $125.00.

Top: Tiered Christmas tree. Various colored rhinestone decorations. $75.00. Middle: Rhinestone ribbon tree, multicolored rhinestones. $80.00. Right: Gold strand, multicolored tree. $75.00.

Left: Candle lantern with enameled holly leaves and red bow. $85.00. Right: St. Nick, emerald green buckle, red rhinestone eyes, pearl trim. $85.00.

Red and aurora borealis rhinestone parure has bracelet, earrings, and necklace. $195.00.

Left: Silver-plated, dark blue rhinestone brooch. $80.00. Right: Blue star brooch. $95.00.

Emerald green parure of brooch, earrings, and ring. Gold-plated. $110.00.

Teal novelty glass stone earrings and bracelet. Trimmed with pearls and blue rhinestones. $105.00.

Left: Lime green rhinestones fill leaf outlines. Brooch. $45.00. Top: Small flower buds filled with pastel rhinestones, green enameled leaf. $95.00. Right: Twin lime green rhinestone flowers, faceted center stone, brooch. $55.00.

Top left: Japanned red rhinestone cherry, enamel leaves. $50.00. Top right: Japanned red rhinestone flower head. $75.00. Bottom: Japanned red rhinestone flower. $60.00.

Pastel parure has two bracelet styles, earrings, and necklace. $300.00.

Left: Lime green brooch and necklace. $160.00. Right: Pink, blue, and lavender rhinestone earrings and necklace. $140.00.

Top left: Blue and lavender rhinestones, pearls, and opalene cabochon butterfly. $125.00. Top right: Silver-plated, blue rhinestone butterfly. $80.00. Bottom: Gold-plated owl, red and green rhinestones. $55.00.

Left: Aurora borealis rhinestone brooch. $95.00. Right: Multicolored rhinestones. Glass tourmaline accents. $90.00.

Top: Olive green and orange rhinestone brooch. $60.00. Right: Multicolored rhinestone leaf. $40.00. Bottom: Pink and lavender rhinestone earrings. $35.00.

Top: Pair of scatter pins. $50.00. Bottom left: Pink and green rhinestone brooch with drop. $105.00. Bottom right: Pink rhinestone brooch. $80.00.

Necklace and earrings of clear and yellow rhinestones. $110.00.

Left: Earrings and bracelet, opalene cabochons, lime green rhinestones. $135.00. Right: Aurora borealis bracelet and earrings. $95.00.

Blue rhinestone and seed pearl bracelet and necklace. $165.00.

Left: Blue rhinestone bracelet. $75.00. Right: Shades of blue rhinestone ring. $55.00.

Left: Lavender rhinestone bracelet. $55.00. Middle: Flower brooch and earrings. Large lavender rhinestone centers. $80.00. Right: Two pairs of earrings. $35.00 pair.

Citrine and gold rhinestone necklace, earrings, and two styles of brooches. Parure. $275.00.

Left: Enamel leaves, pink rhinestone flower brooch. $60.00. Middle: Aurora borealis eyes, belly of multicolored crackle glass cat. $80.00. Right: Silver-plated necklace, enamel flowers with clear rhinestone centers. $55.00.

Left: Three bracelets. $60.00 each. Center: Brooch. $75.00. Right: Necklace, large lavender central rhinestone. $95.00. Bottom right: Three multicolored pairs of earrings. $50.00 pair.

Diamente necklace and earrings. $210.00.

Gold-plated, pearl and diamente pear-shaped rhinestone parure of bracelet, earrings, and necklace. $190.00.

Left: Blue rhinestone flower earrings. $50.00. Middle: Two shades of blue rhinestones brooch. $80.00. Right: Blue rhinestone flower earrings. $60.00.

Pastel parure featuring large lavender stones. Brooch, ring, necklace, and earrings. $300.00.

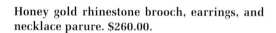

Honey gold rhinestone brooch, earrings, and necklace parure. $260.00.

Pink rhinestones and pearl earrings. These match necklace at bottom of next page. $75.00.

Left: Emerald green rhinestone earrings. $55.00. Middle: Lime green rhinestone necklace and earrings. $145.00. Right: Green rhinestone spray. $80.00.

Left: Lavender rhinestone and pearl earrings. $68.00. Middle: Pink rhinestone and pearl necklace. (Matching earrings priced separately on page 140.) $85.00. Right: Lavender rhinestone and pearl earrings. $65.00.

Enamel flowers accent all three pieces. Left: Emerald green rhinestone brooch. $95.00. Center: Sapphire blue rhinestone earrings. $60.00. Right: Lavender rhinestone brooch. $95.00.

Top left: Lime green rhinestone brooch. $65.00. Top right: Pair of pink rhinestone scatter pins. $80.00. Bottom: Gold rhinestone and pearl earrings, matching brooch. $95.00 set.

Honey gold rhinestone parure of brooch, necklace, and earrings. $195.00.

Multi-grand parure. Two styles of bracelets, brooches, and earrings accompanied by ring and necklace. Features pink, lavender, and clear rhinestones. $2,500.00.

Top: Dark green rhinestones and pearls necklace. $110.00.
Bottom: Lime green rhinestones and pearls necklace.
$110.00.

Pastel parure of necklace, earrings, and bracelet. $195.00.

Parure of ring, earrings, and bracelet featuring lavender rhinestones. $250.00.

Matching earrings and ring, blue stones. $105.00.

Top left: Small pastel brooch. $35.00. Top right: Pastel necklace. $85.00. Bottom: Emerald green rhinestone and pearl earrings. $55.00.

Bracelet and brooch. Rhinestones range in color from pink to amethyst. $95.00.

From left: Emerald green rhinestone bracelet. $55.00. Dark green rhinestone earrings. $45.00. Bracelet of pink rhinestones and pearls. $55.00. Pink rhinestone earrings. $35.00.

Left: Gold rhinestone bracelet. $70.00.
Right: Aurora borealis earrings and
bracelet. $85.00.

Left: Olive green rhinestones, crackle novelty glass,
gold chain tassel. $85.00. Top: Turquoise shells and
blue rhinestones on silver-plated brooch. $110.00.
Bottom: Aurora borealis swirl brooch. $65.00.

Left: Two rings. $40.00 each. Middle: Pearl with gold-
en rhinestone bracelet. $45.00. Right: Silver-plated
star, blue rhinestone earrings. $40.00.

Left: Golden rhinestone spray brooch. $65.00.
Right: Same design brooch in aurora borealis
rhinestones. $50.00

Top: Diamente rhinestone brooch matches earrings at left. $85.00 set. Middle: Small brooch
with pearls, aurora borealis and multicolored
rhinestones with matching earrings. $85.00 set.

Top left: Aurora borealis brooch. $50.00. Top right:
Silver-plated ribbon bow, blue rhinestone brooch.
$35.00. Bottom left: Same design brooch with gold-
plated ribbon, pink rhinestones. $35.00. Bottom right:
Shades of pink and lavender rhinestones spray
brooch. $55.00.

Weiss

History
Began: 1942
Closed: 1971
Designer: Albert Weiss
Signed: Weiss in cartouche
Weiss
Weiss with a copyright in cartouche
Weiss with copyright symbol

Characteristics
Smoky rhinestones
Christmas trees
Eisenberg icing
Long-stemmed flowers

Albert Weiss (pronounced Why-se) learned the basics of costume jewelry at Coro. His years of apprenticeship there helped develop a fine eye for detail that would serve him well when he opened his own business in 1942.

He was both a costume jewelry designer and a manufacturer. His factory was dedicated to hand-set pieces only. In addition he was able to utilize manufacturers in Rhode Island, France, and Germany to fulfill his orders. Realizing the importance of quality rhinestones, Weiss preferred to get his supply from Austria because they gave his jewelry that extra sparkling touch with the higher lead content glass.

When you start to study Weiss and learn his style, you will probably think you have spotted a Weiss for sale, only to turn it over and find there's no logo. Your instinct was probably right, as Weiss manufactured jewelry for wholesale to stores such as J.C. Penney and Sears & Roebuck. The stores would nestle the jewelry in their own presentation boxes for retail sales.

He introduced the gray rhinestone that started the Black Diamond trend. The smoky colored rhinestones became popular, and other companies were soon offering their own versions incorporating the gray stone.

Taking another chance, he designed a series of Christmas trees and had them made in Germany. Bearing the Weiss logo, they soon became bestsellers in America. Imitation must truly be the highest form of flattery since almost all jewelry firms followed in his footsteps and offered Christmas trees in their lines. Once again Weiss was a trendsetter.

When Albert Weiss retired, he left his company in the good hands of his son Michael, a second generation legacy that occurs frequently in the jewelry industry.

The depressed jewelry market brought about the demise of the Weiss Company, and Michael closed the doors in 1971. The company was only three decades in business, but what a wonderful 30 years!

Left: Pink cabochon bracelet, two sizes of brooch, and earrings. Pink rhinestone four-piece parure. $250.00 set. Right: Pink rhinestone bracelet and earrings. $110.00 set.

Lime green and aurora borealis parure of necklace, brooch, and earrings. $225.00.

Top: Blue rhinestone necklace and earrings. $180.00. Bottom: Cuff bracelet in two shades of blue rhinestones. $75.00.

Topaz and brown rhinestone parure of bracelet, necklace, brooch, and earrings. $250.00.

Left: Citrine rhinestone earrings and bracelet. $80.00. Right: Citrine earrings and necklace. $95.00.

Silver filigree leaves, blue and green crystals, aurora borealis rhinestones parure. Bracelet, brooch, and earrings. $195.00.

Amethyst rhinestone parure of bracelet, brooch, and earrings. Pavé diamente rhinestone icing (ribbon). $225.00.

Blue rhinestone parure necklace, bracelet, and earrings. $275.00.

Black and clear rhinestone parure. Bracelet, necklace, brooch, and earrings. $295.00.

Gold rhinestone parure of brooch, earrings, and bracelet. $210.00.

Smoky rhinestone parure bracelet, necklace, and earrings. $320.00.

Left: Diamente rhinestone necklace, bracelet, crescent brooch (middle top), and blossom earrings (middle bottom). Complete parure. $190.00. Center: Diamente rhinestone brooch and earrings (bottom right). $110.00.

Smoky parure of bracelet, brooch, and earrings. $280.00.

Blue rhinestone parure of brooch, earrings, and bracelet. $275.00.

151

Three shades of blue rhinestones, olive green and clear rhinestone necklace and earrings. $165.00.

Left: Diamente rhinestone necklace and earrings. $95.00. Middle: Red and aurora borealis rhinestone necklace and earrings. $105.00. Right: Purple rhinestone necklace. $90.00.

Boxed gold rhinestone necklace and earrings. $110.00.

Diamente rhinestone necklace and drop earrings. $350.00.

Left: Diamente rhinestone bib necklace. $275.00. Right: Diamente rhinestone bracelet. $195.00.

Antique gold bracelet and necklace, orange rhinestones. $165.00.

Left: Lavender bead, clear rhinestone necklace. $90.00. Middle: Red and purple rhinestone necklace. $95.00. Right: Light blue rhinestone necklace. $105.00.

Left: Gold-plated, ruby rhinestone brooch and earrings. $80.00. Right: Green, citrine, and clear rhinestone brooch with green faceted center crystal and matching earrings. $95.00.

Left: On-point square of olive green, gold, and aurora borealis rhinestones and orange cabochon. Earrings below. $90.00 set. Right: Enamel leaf brooch and earrings. $60.00.

Left: On-point square decorated with two shades of blue rhinestone, light blue earrings. $85.00. Right: Teal blue and pink rhinestone brooch and earrings. $160.00.

Left: Diamente rhinestone brooch and earrings. $75.00. Middle: Diamente rhinestone brooch and earrings. $80.00. Right: Diamente rhinestone brooch and earrings. $90.00.

Top: Pair of aurora borealis rhinestone strawberry brooches. $95.00. Left: Enamel apple. $48.00. Right: Red and green rhinestone strawberry brooch and earrings. $145.00.

Top: Gold rhinestone sun brooch and earrings (bottom, left). $85.00. Bottom: Novelty faceted crystal brooch and earrings. $60.00.

Top left: Pink and clear rhinestone brooch. $125.00. Top right: Lime green and clear rhinestone brooch. $130.00. Bottom center: Green and aurora borealis rhinestone brooch. Matching earrings. $105.00.

Left: Blue, red, purple and clear rhinestone brooch and earrings. $185.00. Right: Japanned, plated, shades of blue rhinestones brooch and earrings. $160.00.

Left: Light green and clear rhinestone brooch and earrings. $95.00. Middle: Red rhinestone cross brooch and earrings. $75.00. Right: Olive and green dark green rhinestone Maltese cross brooch and drop earrings. $80.00.

Three sizes of Christmas trees with matching earrings. $550.00 for entire ensemble.

Left: Tree brooch with various colored rhinestone ornaments and earrings. $135.00. Right: Gold tree brooch with rhinestone ornaments. $70.00.

Top: Red and aurora borealis rhinestone tree. $75.00. Middle: Tree with red and clear candle rhinestones. $110.00. Bottom: Green enamel and gold tree. $55.00.

Clockwise from left: Enamel wreath, clear and red rhinestones. $120.00. Lantern, rhinestone candle. $110.00. Poinsettia, enamel and pink rhinestones. $80.00. Gold bells, aurora borealis clapper, gold bow with rhinestone center. $75.00.

Left: Candy cane, clear, green, and red rhinestones. $70.00. Middle: Santa Claus. Red, clear, and green rhinestones. $80.00. Right: Angel, pearl halo. $65.00.

Left: Tourmaline glass brooch and earrings. $85.00. Middle: Enamel orchid and earrings. Features faceted citrine glass stone. $110.00. Right: Twin tourmaline glass flowers and earrings. $80.00.

Left: Diamente rhinestone brooch and earrings. $78.00. Middle: Diamente rhinestone, and three faux pearl brooch and earrings. $180.00. Right: Diamente rhinestone brooch and earrings. $80.00.

Left: White and black navette brooch and earrings. $85.00. Right: Antique gold with fuchsia beads and red glass stones. $170.00.

Left: Shades of orange to brown rhinestone brooch and earrings. $145.00. Middle: Root beer rhinestone brooch and earrings with icing swirls. $135.00. Right: Gold and brown stones, root beer, aurora borealis rhinestone brooch and earrings. $130.00.

Left: Dark blue rhinestone brooch and earrings. $165.00. Middle: Frosted cabochons, blue rhinestone brooch and earrings. $130.00. Right: Blue and green rhinestone, japanned finish brooch and earrings. $165.00.

Top: Pale green and yellow glass stones, Peking glass center brooch and earrings. $85.00. Bottom: Gold rhinestone four-leaf clover and earrings. $70.00.

159

Bridges of clear rhinestone, red glass navettes brooch
and earrings. $300.00.

Left: Red glass stones, tourmaline stone center brooch and earrings. $165.00.
Right: Gold-plated, red rhinestone brooch and earrings. $135.00.

160

Top: Black Maltese cross and earrings. $110.00. Bottom: Owl brooch and earrings. $135.00.

Left: Long-stemmed peach and brown glass stone flower with earrings. $150.00. Right: Green and orange flower and earrings. $130.00.

Top left: Yellow stone, white petal blossom with ladybug. $45.00. Top right: White stone flower with pavé rhinestone leaves. $50.00. Bottom left: White glass stones, red cabochon center, red and green rhinestone stem and leaves. $105.00. Bottom right: White glass petals, black cabochon center earrings. $40.00.

Left: Topaz and orange rhinestone flower. $55.00. Middle: Orange and brown glass flower. $40.00. Right: Citrine and brown flower. $38.00.

Top: Pink and purple flower. $80.00. Bottom left: Green rhinestones topped with enamel flower earrings. $75.00. Bottom right: Lavender glass flower earrings. $45.00.

Top: Enamel butterfly. $68.00. Bottom left: Blue glass stone flower. $55.00. Bottom right: Frosted blue petals, blue cabochon flower. $60.00.

Top left: Gold and red rhinestone butterfly. $150.00. Top right: Japanned finish, red and black rhinestone pair of butterflies. $110.00. Bottom: Novelty striped glass stone butterfly. $155.00.

Top: Gold braid outline butterfly filled with pink rhinestones, matching earrings. $225.00. Bottom: Pastel, multicolored rhinestone butterfly and earrings. $225.00.

Top: Green rhinestone butterfly. $110.00. Left: Red and blue rhinestone butterfly. $95.00. Bottom right: Pink enamel frame butterfly with pink rhinestones and earrings. $145.00.

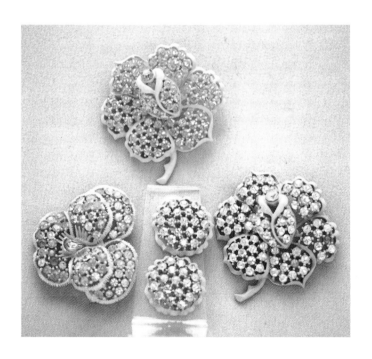

Top: Pink enamel frame rose brooch filled with pink rhinestones. $80.00. Bottom left: Pink enamel frame pansy, pastel rhinestones. $85.00. Bottom right: Blue enamel frame rose filled with citrine and blue rhinestones, matching earrings. $125.00.

Top left: Pink rhinestone bow. $75.00. Top right: Peking glass center, with faux pearl brooch $55.00. Bottom left: Gold rhinestone four-leaf clover. $40.00. Bottom right: Enamel blue flower on Weiss card. $95.00.

Clockwise from top left: Pink enamel flower. $55.00.
Yellow enamel flower. $55.00. Lavender violet. $60.00.
Enamel orchid. $75.00.

Left: Shades of brown rhinestone brooch. $150.00. Top:
Blue glass, pavé ribbons of diamente rhinestones. $135.00.
Bottom: Two shades of green rhinestones Maltese cross,
gold edges. $45.00.

Left: Shades of pink and red rhinestone brooch.
$150.00. Top: Copper-plated, bronze and aurora
borealis rhinestone bow. $70.00. Bottom: Olive
green glass cabochons, pink and purple rhinestones, two gold leaves. $110.00.

Top: Amethyst rhinestone brooch. $110.00. Left:
Aurora borealis brooch. $80.00. Right: Blue and
clear rhinestone brooch. $110.00.

Left: Diamente and emerald green rhinestone brooch. $225.00. Right: Orange rhinestones, dark green glass stones, japanned finish. $375.00.

Top left: Black enamel heart. $45.00. Top right: Blue cabochon, blue and silver rhinestones. $110.00. Center: Gold and diamente rhinestone leaf. $50.00. Bottom left: Shades of pink rhinestones. $90.00. Bottom right: Frosted white and blue stones, clear rhinestones. $105.00.

Top: Hand-blown pink blossoms, pink rhinestone brooch. $275.00. Bottom: Red and blue cabochon crown with faux pearls. $325.00.

Top: Multicolored cabochon brooch. $50.00. Bottom left: Artist palette of multicolored rhinestones. $175.00. Bottom right: Faux pearl and jade Maltese cross. $110.00.

Clockwise from top: Enamel and pink rhinestone blossoms. $65.00. Blue enamel and rhinestone pansy. $85.00. Enamel pink blossom with pink and red rhinestones. $70.00. Enamel leaves, multicolored flower bud. $80.00.

Clockwise from top: Metallic body, gold rhinestone winged inset. $70.00. Japanned finish, dark blue aurora borealis and rhinestone insect. $95.00. Green cabochon body, green rhinestone head and body. $85.00.

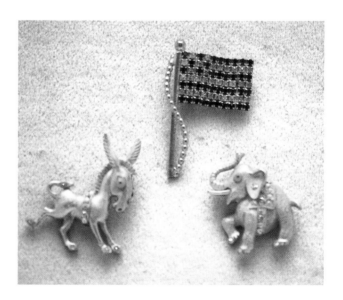

Patriotic trio. Top: Flag. $90.00. Bottom: Democratic and Republican party symbols. $150.00 pair.

166

Clockwise from top left: Green and yellow enamel bug studded with rhinestones. $65.00. Cream and green enamel bug with green rhinestones. $68.00. Enamel bug with spread wings. $75.00. Pink enamel frog with green spots. $80.00.

Left: Faceted green body, enamel winged insect. $70.00. Right: Enameled owl. $55.00. Bottom: Green cabochon tie tack. $55.00.

Left: Carded enamel toucan. $75.00. Middle: In original box, silver-plated brooch and earrings. Blue rhinestones. $125.00. Right: Carded starfish, shades of red rhinestones. $80.00.

Four bracelets. $65.00 to $80.00 each.

From left: Diamente rhinestone bracelet. $130.00. Eight rows of diamente rhinestones, three rows of blue glass stones. Bracelet. $295.00. Blue rhinestone flower bracelet. $125.00. Dark topaz stones, gold leaves, aurora borealis and brown rhinestone bracelet. $105.00.

Ten assorted pairs of earrings. $48.00 to 65.00 pair.

The Three Kings

Trifari

History

Began: 1918
Still in production
Designers: Alfred Philippe
Andre Boeuf
Signed: KTF – 1935
Trifari with a crown 1930s
Trifari with crown and copyright symbol
Diane

Characteristics

Swarovski multicolored rhinestones
Plating that looks like real gold
Lucite sterling animals (1942)
Gold/pearl line

The three men who were to be named the "Rhinestone Kings" did not realize the part they would play in history. Gustavo Trifari was a manufacturer and designer of intricate hair ornaments and bar pins back in 1918. One of his biggest competitors employed a record-breaking salesman Leo Krussman.

The jewelry industry is a close knit family, and each man was aware of the other's skills. The two joined those skills in 1924 and brought in partner Carl Fishel in 1925.

Trifari/Krussman/Fishel were the first to use imported Austrian multicolored rhinestones, earning them the title of Rhinestone Kings.

Joining the trio in 1930 was designer Alfred Philippe, who had been a valuable designer with Van Cleef and Arpel and at Cartier Jewelers. As the head designer for Trifari, he initiated the practice of using multicolored Swarovski rhinestones and hand-setting them.

His designs were the creation of a jeweler who thought in terms of diamonds, rubies, and emeralds then finalized the piece in high-quality rhinestones that rivaled the natural gems. Years of training had developed his jeweler's skills, allowing his artistic designs to be brought to life in the rhinestone world.

The kings were the first fashion jewelry company to advertise nationally, and their slogan was "Jewels by Trifari" with a crown trademark in 1938.

Earlier pieces were marked TKF for the three partners, but they decided to eliminate the use of the initials and opted to use the more French sounding name of Trifari, which has been in use ever since.

In 1940 they introduced their crown line in honor of the coronation of Queen Elizabeth. Their Providence plant converted most of its manpower to the war efforts during World War II. Through negotiations with the Royal Air Force in England, they obtained the exclusive rights to their emblem. The resulting brooch was worn by sweethearts, wives, and mothers of those brave men who had joined the British Royal Air Force. All sales proceeds were donated to the British War Fund.

As part of their contribution to the war efforts, Trifari installed Plexiglas windshields and turrets in military bombers. The slightest flaw in the material could not be tolerated, and flawed glass would go to the scrap pile. Alfred Philippe had the creative genius and imagination to utilize this rejected material. Noticing the stack and the thickness of the product, he had cabochons cut. This design triumph was the Clear Line, whimsical animal jewelry to put a smile on the faces of war-weary women. The clear or "jelly belly" stone is the predominant feature of the animal. Swordfish danced, fish swam, spiders crawled, and flies flew in these whimsical Trifari darlings. The three very wise men were regally the epitome of the fashion jewelry industry, filling the wants and desires of the rich and famous while offering the average housewife fine quality jewelry for moderate prices.

But perhaps the most historically important impact was their legal battle for copyright protection. They were instrumental in getting Congress to recognize the artistic values of fashion jewelry designs. This American art form was formally recognized with the 1954 Copyright Law protecting the artist's rights.

After Trifari was purchased by Hallmark in the late 1970s, three of the top designers were featured on the jewelry, in a rare tribute recognizing them for their contributions to the world of costume jewelry. A larger oval will have the name of Kunio Mataumo (jewelry designer), Marsha Breslow (handbag) or Marcella Solz (pocketbook and accessories). (See bottom photo, page 173.)

The firm of Trifari has been sold and resold and is now located in Puerto Rico.

Left: Diamente rhinestone and gold-plated parure of brooch, necklace, and earrings. $225.00. Right: Floral diamente rhinestone and gold-plated parure of brooch, necklace, and earrings. $250.00.

Diamente rhinestones in various shapes, parure of necklace, brooch, and earrings. $250.00.

170

Diamente chaton rhinestone parure earrings, bracelet, and necklace. $225.00.

Flower parure, necklace, brooch, and earrings. $250.00.

Diamente rhinestone grape cluster parure. Necklace, stick pin, and earrings. $295.00.

Silver-plated leaf parure necklace, bracelet, and earrings. $190.00

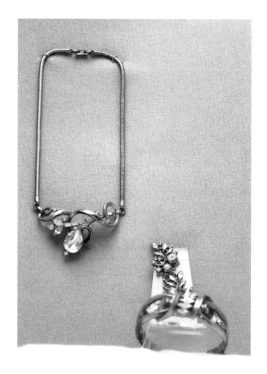

Gold-plated diamente rhinestone parure, necklace, earrings, and bracelet. $200.00.

Silver-plated diamente rhinestone parure, earrings, necklace, and bracelet. $195.00.

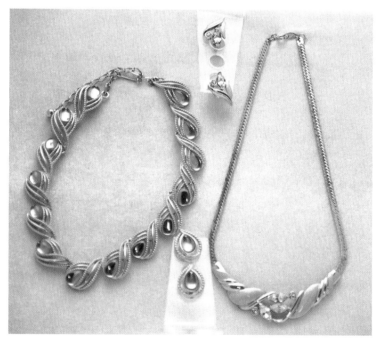

Gold-plated red rhinestone parure, necklace, earrings, and bracelet. $275.00.

Left: Pink moonstone necklace and earrings. $110.00. Right: Pink enamel necklace and earrings. $95.00.

Left: Silver flower necklace and earrings. $90.00.
Middle: Pearl and silver parure, necklace, bracelet, and earrings. $175.00.

Left: Enamel white leaves and blue flowers with diamente rhinestone necklace and earrings. $175.00. Right: Pink plastic and diamente rhinestone parure of necklace, bracelet, and earrings. $210.00

Left: Marked Mataumo parure, necklace bracelet, and earrings. $300.00.
Right: Pink plastic parure, necklace, bracelet, and earrings. $160.00.

Left: Gold matte finish with silver leaves earrings and bracelet. $120.00. Middle: Faux turquoise and pearl bracelet. $65.00. Right: Lime green rhinestone necklace and earrings. $90.00.

Left: White plastic necklace and earrings. $80.00. Middle: Woven white plastic on-point square necklace. $45.00. Right: Seed pearl bracelet and necklace. $100.00.

Left and bottom: Silver-plated blue rhinestone bracelet and necklace. $110.00. Right top: Silver basket with dark blue rhinestone brooch. $85.00.

Rhinestone studded faux pearl necklace and brooch. $205.00.

Red rhinestone, gold-plated earrings and necklace. $190.00.

Triple strand faux pearl necklace and earrings. $140.00.

Left: Frosted crystals, green rhinestone earrings and necklace. $145.00. Right: Red and diamente rhinestone earrings and necklace. $180.00.

Six strand green beads and crystals necklace and earrings. $80.00.

Left: Filigree gold and diamente rhinestone earrings and neck-lace. $150.00. Right: Gold-plated rhinestone baguettes neck-lace and earrings. $175.00.

Left: Silver-plated blue moonstone necklace and earrings. Note paper hang tag. $90.00. Right: Silver-plated diamente rhinestones necklace and earrings. $85.00.

Left: Red enamel and gold-plated snake earrings and bracelet. $180.00. Right: Gold-plated cuff bracelet. $125.00.

Blossoms bear the name of design-er Mataumo. Necklace. $45.00.

Left: Faux jade necklace and brooch. $160.00. Right: Silver-plated blue rhinestone necklace and earrings. $98.00.

Triple silver chain necklace and earrings. Amethyst glass stones. $200.00.

Left: White glass petals necklace and earrings. $65.00. Right: White petal necklace. $40.00.

Top left: White novelty glass, silver-plated brooch. $55.00. Top middle: Gold and white enamel brooch. $40.00. Bottom left: Enamel daisy earrings. $35.00. Bottom middle and right: White enamel leaves, blue rhinestone flowers earrings and necklace. $110.00.

Left: White enamel necklace. $135.00. Right: White enamel bow brooch and earrings. $80.00.

Top: Gold collar with faux coral and turquoise stones. $110.00. Bottom: Imitation turquoise bead necklace. $80.00.

Left: Pearl and smoky rhinestone necklace. $250.00. Right top: Silver-plated blue rhinestone necklace. $90.00. Right bottom: Opalene stones, green rhinestone necklace. $200.00.

Assortment of necklaces. $110.00 – 150.00 each.

Silver snake chain, pave diamente rhinestone leaves, red crystal petal necklace. $450.00.

Left: Scarab enamel necklace. $85.00. Top right: Sweater guard. $45.00. Middle right: Sweater guard and earrings, diamente rhinestones. $68.00.

Top: "Jelly belly" spider. $575.00. Bottom: "Jelly belly" earrings and fly. $750.00.

Chess set, King, Queen, and Rook fur clips. Matching earrings. $650.00.

Top: Red cabochon body bird. $70.00. Bottom left: Blue moonstone earrings and bird. $100.00. Bottom right: Gold-plated owl. $48.00.

Top left and right: Matching royal scepters. Opalescent stones, red, green, and clear rhinestones. $180.00 each. Top middle: Smallest crown, clear and blue rhinestones. $85.00. Center: Sword with red and blue cabochons, matching crown at left, earrings bottom left. Complete set $550.00. Bottom right: Silver-plated crown, red, green, blue, and clear rhinestones. $225.00.

Left: Blue sapphire and diamente rhinestone brooch and earrings. $180.00. Right: Citrine and blue rhinestone brooch. $80.00.

Left: Pavé diamente rhinestone leaf brooch and earrings. $135.00. Right: Lavender and amethyst rhinestone flowers, clear rhinestone brooch and earrings. $160.00.

Left: Silver-plated bow and earrings. $80.00. Right: Matte silver-plated brooch and earrings. $70.00.

Left: Faux pearl center, lavender, gold, and citrine rhinestone brooch and earrings. $150.00. Right: Gold Christmas star brooch and earrings. $140.00.

From left: Red and clear rhinestone brooch and earrings. $250.00. Pavé clear rhinestone brooch. $195.00. Diamente rhinestone brooch and earrings. $145.00.

Left: Two shades green rhinestone bracelet and earrings. $140.00. Right: Pastel rhinestone floral brooch and earrings. $95.00.

Left: Swirls of citrine and diamente rhinestone brooch and earrings. $110.00. Middle: Faux sapphire star brooch and earrings. $125.00. Right: Citrine, blue, and clear rhinestone brooch and earrings. $150.00.

Left: Pink and clear moonstone brooch and earrings. $95.00. Middle: Citrine rhinestone brooch and earrings. $130.00. Right: Silver-plated diamente rhinestone brooch and earrings. $175.00.

Left: Silver-plated pink, blue, and clear rhinestone brooch and earrings. $140.00. Right: Gold-plated diamente rhinestone brooch and earrings. $95.00.

Left: Dark green rhinestone brooch and earrings. $140.00. Middle: Golden yellow and diamente rhinestone four-leaf clover brooch with earrings. $95.00. Right: Silver-plated faux pearl brooch and earrings. $125.00.

Clockwise from top: Gold leaf and pearl circular brooch. $45.00. Gold golf clubs, pearl ball. $80.00. Pearl and gold brooch and earrings. $65.00. Wishbone with pearl. $45.00

Clockwise from top left: Faux pearl and gold leaf brooch and earrings. $80.00. Faux pearl brooch. $35.00. Faux pearl nosegay. $65.00. Gold-plated basket of pearl flowers brooch. $40.00.

Top left: Diamente rhinestone duette. $85.00. Top right: Diamente rhinestone duette. $85.00. Bottom left: Pink crystal beads, diamente rhinestone twin fur clips without frame. $65.00. Middle and right: Duette frame that accommodates twin rhinestone clips. $105.00.

Left: Faux pearl and clear rhinestone brooch and earrings. $85.00. Right: Gold-plated bracelet and earrings, clear rhinestones. $70.00.

Left: Faux pearl, clear rhinestones, and red enamel brooch. $160.00. Right: Pavé diamente rhinestone floral brooch. $195.00. Bottom: Red enamel hyacinths brooch. $340.00.

Top: Amethyst cabochons, pavé diamente rhinestone butterfly. $180.00. Bottom: Red enameled tulip. $205.00.

Left: Enamel nosegay fur clip. $250.00. Middle: Diamente rhinestone exotic bird. $350.00. Right: Enamel carnation fur clip. $375.00.

Clockwise from top left: Enamel flower, faux pearl brooch. $85.00. Faux pearls, pavé diamente rhinestone center, and enamel leaves. $90.00. Enamel lily of the valley fur clip. $300.00. Pavé diamente rhinestone lilies, enameled fur clip. $350.00.

Clockwise from top left: Basket of pink enameled flowers, clear rhinestone centers. $48.00. White enamel flower. $70.00. Red enamel flower, white chalk bead center. $55.00. Enamel dogwood blossom. $45.00.

Clockwise from top left: Gold-plated clear rhinestones and topaz crystals brooch. $80.00. Faux turquoise beads, enamel leaves. $45.00. Enamel and clear rhinestone flower brooch. $160.00. Faux ruby crystals, diamente rhinestone bouquet. $325.00.

Clockwise from top: Ruby, diamente, and emerald green rhinestone brooch. $160.00. Pink rhinestone brooch. $90.00. Two shades of blue rhinestones, silver plated brooch. $95.00. Silver-plated, blue and clear rhinestones. $125.00.

Clockwise from top right: Lime green crystals, green navettes brooch. $110.00. Red and clear rhinestone brooch. $95.00. Sapphire and clear rhinestone brooch. $150.00. Pale blue crystals, aurora borealis rhinestones brooch. $90.00.

Left: Silver frond with pearls. $105.00. Right: Gold pod with faux pearl peas. $180.00.

Left: Citrine and topaz rhinestone floral brooch. $145.00. Middle: Citrine and clear rhinestone brooch. $85.00. Right: Topaz, clear, and golden yellow rhinestone brooch. $90.00.

Top: Silver-plated blue rhinestone brooch. $95.00. Left: Blue and diamente rhinestone brooch. $105.00 Right: Silver-plated blue rhinestone three-leaf clover brooch. $70.00.

Left: Opalene navettes, blue rhinestones brooch. $125.00. Right: Gold-plated clear rhinestone swag brooch. $45.00. Bottom: Gold-plated diamente rhinestone brooch. $60.00.

Clockwise from top: Gold-plated leaf, clear rhinestone brooch. $95.00. Gold-plated clear rhinestone brooch. $60.00. Gold-plated leaf, clear rhinestones. $60.00. Gold-plated bow, clear rhinestone brooch. $80.00.

Left: Enamel and clear rhinestone brooch. $195.00. Top: Gold-plated clear rhinestone leaf brooch. $80.00. Right: Black enameling, Pavé diamente rhinestones. $140.00.

Gold-plated zodiac brooches, Taurus and Leo. $35.00 each.

Left: Gold-plated pavé diamente rhinestones and faux pearl. $95.00. Middle: Gold-plated faux pearl center brooch. $65.00. Right: Gold-plated leaf, faux pearls. $40.00.

Clockwise from top: Cherub. $90.00. Wreath, green and red rhinestones. $85.00. Older scarecrow man. $85.00. Scarecrow man and woman. $200.00 pair.

Clockwise from top: Blue, green, and clear rhinestone mythical bird. $90.00. Pave diamente rhinestone horse. $100.00. Enameled fox hunter on pavé diamente rhinestone horse. $180.00. Faux pearl poodle. $35.00. Green cabochon belly rabbit. $35.00. Faux turquoise belly, blue cabochon eyes dog. $45.00.

Top: Pavé diamente rhinestone wings, gold-plated insect. $160.00. Left: Gold duckling. $60.00. Right: Gold elephant. $80.00.

Clockwise from top left: Enamel seahorse, faux pearls and clear rhinestones. $295.00. Lavender and clear rhinestone fish with amethyst cabochon belly, enamel fins. $125.00. Red enamel lobster. $95.00. Enamel and clear rhinestone fish. $150.00.

White enamel quartet. Clockwise from top: Enamel owl, cabochon eyes. $130.00. Enamel duckling. $145.00. Enamel horse. $140.00. Enamel cat. $125.00.

Left: Enamel lizard. $50.00. Right: Enamel ginkgo leaf, clear rhinestone bug. $180.00. Bottom: Snail. $90.00.

Top: Mother Goose, diamente rhinestones. $145.00. Left: Gold-plated lion, mane of diamente rhinestones. $180.00. Right: Gold-plated lobster. $90.00.

Clockwise from top left: Gold-plated bird. $180.00. Blue cabochon belly bird. $125.00. Blue belly frog. $110.00. Red white rhinestone, blue cabochon bird. $125.00. Enamel bug. $65.00.

Top: Two sizes of gold butterflies with diamente rhinestones. Earrings to match. $250.00. Bottom right: Gold and diamente rhinestone butterfly. $90.00.

Clockwise from top left: Black enamel butterfly. $135.00. Red and clear rhinestone butterfly. $150.00. Faux turquoise dragonfly $110.00. Faux turquoise butterfly. $130.00.

Clockwise from top: RAF wings. Diamente rhinestone brooch. $250.00. Red, white, and blue rhinestone sweetheart brooch. $150.00. Red and blue enamel, clear rhinestone Christian symbol brooch. $125.00. Diamente rhinestone sword. $80.00.

Left: Faux pearl heads, clear rhinestone Cossack dancers. $290.00 pair. Middle: Ballerina, green and clear rhinestones. $195.00. Right: Ballerina, clear rhinestones. $140.00.

Clockwise from top left: Green and red rhinestones, gold-plated fleur-de-lis. $105.00. Green and red fruit salad stones, clear rhinestones. $110.00. Green cabochon, red and green rhinestone, pearl row. $110.00. Turquoise bracelet. $110.00.

Left: Black enamel, pavé diamente rhinestone bracelet and brooch. $235.00. Center: Pavé diamente rhinestone orchid, red baguettes. $275.00. Right: Pavé diamente rhinestone brooch. $150.00.

Left: Earrings and bracelet, clear rhinestones. $115.00. Center: Clear rhinestone bracelet and earrings. $98.00. Right: Brooch and bracelet, gold-plated leaves, faux pearls, and clear rhinestones. $165.00.

Left: Earrings and bracelet. Red rhinestones, gold-plated. $165.00. Right: Gold-plated clear rhinestones brooch and earrings. $90.00.

Left: Diamente and sapphire rhinestone bracelet. $125.00. Middle trio: Pavé diamente rhinestone and blue rhinestones. $150.00 each. Right: Clear rhinestone silver-plated bracelet. $85.00.

From left: Gold filigree bracelet. $65.00. Next: Gold and clear rhinestone bracelet. $80.00. Next: Gold leaves, clear rhinestone bracelet. $95.00. Bottom: Articulated topaz rhinestone bracelet. $110.00.

Ten pairs of earrings. $40.00 – 50.00 each. Bottom left: Large, emerald cut topaz ring. $90.00.

Left: QVC green enamel and red rhinestone holly tree. $65.00. Right: QVC Lucite belly bird. $70.00.

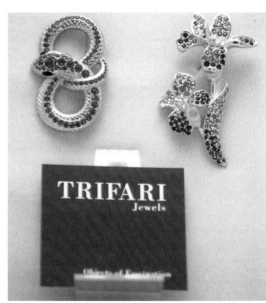

Left: QVC snake, red rhinestones. $80.00. Right: QVC iris, pink, lavender, and green rhinestones. $110.00.

194

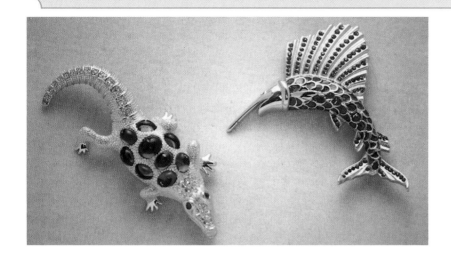

Left: QVC alligator, green cabochons. $95.00. Right: QVC enameled sword-fish. Green and red stones on tail and fins. $125.00.

Trifari Safari, QVC. Left: Leopard. $165.00. Right: Black enamel, red rhinestone giraffe. $165.00.

Top: Lion head, pavé diamente rhinestones. $140.00. Left: Carded unicorn, pavé diamente rhinestones. $150.00. Center: Exotic bird, clear, red, and blue rhinestones. $125.00. Right: Black enamel cat head earrings. $45.00.

Trifari Safari, QVC. Zebra head, green cabochon. $150.00.

Men of Distinction

The strong personalities of the different designers showed in the jewelry they created. There are many men who could be classified as men of distinction, and it was hard for me to just select just a few.

I chose four of my own favorites. After reading their stories and examining pictures of their jewelry, you will also certainly acquire an appreciation for their artistry.

Barclay Jewelry Inc.

History

Began: 1940s
Closed: 1950s
Designers: Unknown
Signed: Barclay
Manufacturer: Rice Weiner

Characteristics

Pastel-colored rhinestones
Numerous small rhinestones
Circular pattern design
Antique gold finish

Barclay Jewelry Inc. was a Providence, Rhode Island firm dating back to the late 1940s and into the 1950s. Their showroom was located on Fifth Avenue in New York. The company concentrated on making costume jewelry that was a fashionable adornment for women with a modest spending budget. Barclay produced a line of earrings, bracelets, necklaces, and chokers in the medium price range.

Their jewelry is always signed simply "Barclay." Their pieces do not command the respect and prices that the name of McClelland Barclay gets in today's market. In looking at the bracelet pictured at top left on page 198, you could almost mistake it for a Hollycraft design.

The grand parure as seen on page 197 (consisting of a ring, necklace, brooch, and earrings) is a fine example of their technique. The earrings were mounted on the original card bearing the Barclay name positioned on a drawing of an artist palette. Each piece of this suite features hand-set multicolored pastel rhinestones of various shapes and sizes. The circles are in two sizes, ¾" and 1¾". The bracelet, earrings, and upper necklace all are composed of the ¾" design. The lower necklace drop was created by using the large circle. The design is carried throughout with a golden twisted braid trimming that unites all the pieces, making this a good example typical of the Barclay jewelry line.

Of course, one could falsely assume that there is a great wall dividing this company from the famed McClelland Barclay, until you see the fur clip at bottom right on page 198. From across the room your first reaction might be excitement — until you have the opportunity to examine it closely. Always turn the jewelry over to look at the underneath side first. The dealer will assume you are checking the name, when in reality you are checking for repairs, worn plating, and construction techniques.

The precise architectural construction of the later company is missing. Turn it over and you will see the cabochons have a depth or full color value but have been glued in with a messy technique that has allowed excess glue to overflow the depressions.

The best way to share your acquired knowledge is to buy the clip so that you can display it alongside a McClelland Barclay piece. To see, feel, touch, and weigh help one become a better shopper.

Parure consisting of necklace (shown at bottom left), brooch, ring, and earrings. Gold-plated circles are repeated in the design, filled with pastel multicolored rhinestones. $175.00.

Gold-plated necklace with two circles. Both are filled with pastel rhinestones and encircled with a twisted braid frame. $90.00.

Gold-plated gold rhinestone anchor with decorative rope. $65.00.

Set of matching ring and earrings. Gold-plated rectangular design is filled with gold and amber rhinestones of various shapes. Twisted braid frame. $95.00.

Small pink chaton rhinestones cluster to form a circle of delight on bracelet and ear-rings. Gold-plated. $90.00 – 100.00.

Left: Silver filigree bracelet with five floral diamente rhinestone designs. Value $55.00. Right: Pair of earrings with red heart-shaped specialty stones. $35.00.

Gold-plated fur clip with green teardrop cabochons. Art Deco floral pattern. $135.00.

McClelland Barclay

History

Began: 1937
Closed: 1943
Designer: McClelland Barclay
Signed: McClelland Barclay
Manufacturer: Rice Weiner

Characteristics

Architectural construction
Masculine, strong lines
Art Deco style
Channeled structure

A faded photograph of a handsome World War II U.S. Naval officer has haunted me since I first saw it. He was dressed in his lieutenant commander uniform, casually leaning against the fireplace mantle with a pipe in one hand, perfect casting for a Hollywood movie, the part of the romantic leading man.

Even his name had a distinguished, refined, elegant English lilt — McClelland Barclay.

Then I was shown a piece of jewelry this man had designed over 50 years ago, and his ghost came back to visit me for he had embodied the necklace with the same strong masculinity.

Take a close look at the picture below. Here are parts of a McClelland brooch that will show how well he built his jewelry, using proven construction methods to create a sturdy base.

Look at the clip at top right on page 200, 2⅜" long by 1¾" wide. It is a heraldic shield of geometric proportions and a true example of his dedication to the Art Deco trend. Well-defined metal sculpture makes a golden frame for the overlay of the third level that bears the diamente and dark blue rhinestones. Remember that the jewelry is always proudly marked with the full name — McClelland Barclay.

He began his life in St. Louis, Missouri, on May 9, 1893, and spent his early school years there. At the age of 16 he moved to Chicago where he was able to attend the Art Institute, then on to the Corcoran Art School in Washington and the Art Students' League in New York.

He was able to extend his studies, working with George Bridgman, H.C. Ives, and Thomas Fogarty. At the age of 19, he began his multi-media artistic career as a designer, sculptor, portrait painter, illustrator, and candlestick maker.

His illustrations could be found on the covers of *Cosmopolitan, Ladies Home Journal, Saturday Evening Post,* and others. The "Fisher Body Girl" was the result of his fine eye for beauty. He was awarded many national prizes for his posters.

McClelland Barclay Arts Products Inc. of New York was formed in 1937 to warehouse the wide range of talents of this artist. Before long, he expanded into designing jewelry for the Rice Weiner Company of Providence, Rhode Island.

Having earned a commission of lieutenant commander in the Naval Reserve, he was quick to volunteer for the draft when the first sounds of battle were heard. Choosing a heroic path for his country, he sealed his fate. On a landing ship in the Pacific he met his fate when a Japanese torpedo struck on July 18, 1943. All hands aboard were declared Missing in Action.

Six short years of his life, 1937 to 1943, were all he had to give to the costume jewelry world, making the search for his jewelry a treasure hunt. Because of his limited production, uncovering one of his artistic jewelry works is indeed worthy to be placed in the pirate's treasure trove. His legacy lives on in his creations.

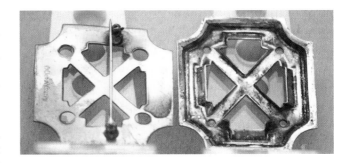

Front and back stamped McClelland Barclay findings show the architectural concepts he used in his jewelry.

Gold-plated circle fur clip with topaz navette rhinestones and furled rows of pavé rhinestones. $450.00.

Gold-plated fur clip, sapphire blue rhinestones seated on pavé diamente heraldic shield. $525.00.

Antique gold-plated double cord tied in a bow knot and each end with a gold cap. $650.00.

Articulated necklace, gold-plated, square ruby rhinestones and diamente pavé trim. $450.00.

Kramer Jewelry Creations

History

Began: 1943
Closed: 1970s
Designer: Louis Kramer
Signed: Kramer
Kramer of NY
Dior by Kramer
Amourelle

Characteristics

Ear cover earrings
Netted rhinestones
1950s "Golden Look"
1960s "Diamond Look"

New York, New York was chosen by Louis Kramer as home for Kramer Jewelry Creations in 1943. How could he ever dream that the company would last 30 years?

Brothers Morris and Harry quickly joined him in developing the company that almost overnight established a high rating in the jewelry industry for quality and design. The brothers created exquisite jewelry that came to the attention of Christian Dior who chose the Kramer company to represent his design house.

In the 1950s, Kramer was responsible for all production of Dior Jewelry in the United States. The Kramer brothers proudly stamped "Dior by Kramer." Their own work was signed Kramer or Kramer of New York and featured both expensive and inexpensive costume jewelry lines.

In the 1950s Kramer introduced the "Golden Look," utilizing the women's fashion trend of tailored suits. The simple lines of the designs brought out the beauty of jewelry so well that it was difficult to tell gold plating from the real thing.

The 1960s gave women the opportunity to flaunt their "diamonds" in Kramer rhinestone creations touted as the "Diamond Look." One of their striking innovations was the "ear cover." The entire ear, revealed by upswept hairdos, glistened with a single unit rhinestone earring. A curved wire tucked behind the top part of the ear with a small clip-back towards the lower curve of the ear.

Kramer's master of design has never been questioned. Who would have thought of putting black net over rhinestones before hand-setting them in their fittings? The rhinestones glow through the net, giving the jewelry the rank of fine evening wear.

In making a silver parure, long-stemmed flowers on slender silver stalks were topped with gleaming rhinestones, gathered into a single container, and placed into a fitting. The nosegays were repeated on the necklace, bracelet, and even on the earrings,

meticulous craftsmanship that is rarely attempted today.

Their glamorous jewelry line was hard hit along with many other similar companies with the advent of the trend-setting natural look. Women were letting their hair down, and casual clothes were in. Little make-up or jewelry was being worn. The back-to-nature fashion trend tolled the doom, and Kramer Jewelry Creations closed its door in the late 1970s.

The brothers' art lives on though as we preserve their artistry in our jewelry boxes and our collections.

Olive green and citrine rhinestone parure of earrings, bracelet, and brooch. $250.00.

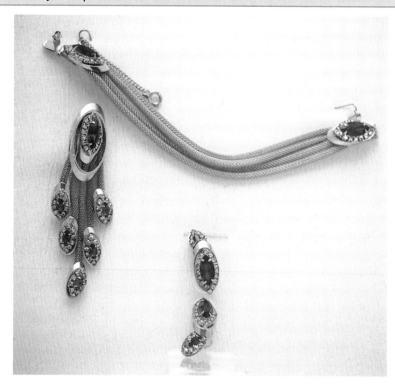

"Golden Look" parure, bracelet, brooch, and earrings. Ruby red and clear rhinestones. $265.00.

Blue and green rhinestone parure of earrings, necklace, and two brooches. $350.00.

Crackle glass parure of bracelet, necklace, and earrings. Blue and green rhinestones. $280.00.

Pink and clear rhinestone parure has necklace, bracelet, and earrings. $225.00.

Blue sapphire cabochons framed with diamente rhinestones. Parure of earrings, necklace, and bracelet. $295.00.

"Diamond Look" necklace, bracelet, and earrings parure. Diamente rhinestones. $210.00.

Left: Gold half balls alternating with diamente rhinestone parure. Necklace, bracelet, brooch, and earrings. $250.00. Right: Gold half balls alternating with sapphire blue rhinestone parure of bracelet, brooch, and earrings. $195.00.

Pink and ruby red rhinestone parure. Necklace, two brooches, bracelet, and earrings. $325.00.

"Diamond Look" parure of necklace, bracelet, and earrings. Various sizes of diamente rhinestones. $240.00.

Left: Diamente baguettes are featured in necklace and earrings. $155.00.
Right: Gold-plated necklace with various shapes of diamente rhinestones that include pavé work. $110.00.

Torsade of pink pearls, crystal beads
necklace and earrings. $295.00.

White chalk beads, silver-plated, and pavé ribbons of
diamente rhinestones in necklace and earrings. $165.00.

Navy blue discs in necklace and earrings. Pearl and
rhinestone ornamentation. $210.00.

Left: Aurora borealis necklace and earrings. $140.00.
Right: Golden rhinestones and necklace combined with
brooch. $235.00.

Diamente ruby red rhinestone necklace and earrings. $300.00.

Left: Black net over topaz rhinestone parure of earrings, necklace, and bracelet. Gold-plated. $375.00. Right: Silver-plated earrings and necklace. Black net over clear rhinestones. $220.00.

Lavender and light blue rhinestone necklace and earrings. $210.00.

"Diamond Lock" necklace and earrings.
$298.00.

Gold-plated necklace utilizes pearls. $88.00.

"Diamond Look" double rhinestone chain necklace.
$310.00.

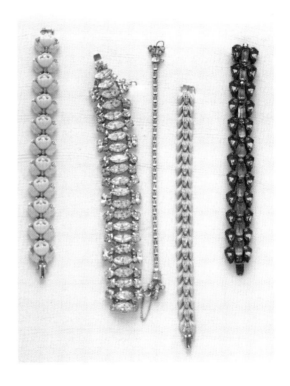

First, from left: Enamel pink bud flower
bracelet. $85.00. Second: Diamente rhinestone
bracelet. $105.00. Third: Diamente tennis
bracelet. $70.00. Fourth: Gold-plated diamente
rhinestones bracelet. $74.00. Fifth: Blue and
green rhinestone bracelet. $110.00.

Left: Yellow to rosy pink rhinestone bracelet has one clear diamente row. Matching earrings add changeling cabochons. $125.00. Right: Clear, citrine, gold, topaz, and bronze rhinestone bracelet and earrings. $110.00.

Clockwise from top: Small diamente rhinestone brooch. $55.00. Diamente rhinestone brooch. $80.00. Five rows of diamente rhinestones bracelet. $98.00. Diamente earrings. $55.00. Tic-tac-toe diamente rhinestone earrings. $68.00.

Day and Night convertible brooch. Night version: Silver-plated brooch with diamente rhinestones. Kramer applied for a patent on this design concept. $200.00.

Day version: Silver-plated brooch becomes a plain daytime brooch by simply turning the outer ring until the rhinestones are concealed from view.

Top: Silver-plated brooch. Branches trimmed with pearls and diamente rhinestones. $55.00. Left: Silver leaf brooch and earrings with diamente rhinestones. $90.00. Right: Leaf brooch, half filled with diamente rhinestones. $68.00.

Left: Fuchsia, lavender, blue, and green rhinestone brooch tied with diamente pavé rhinestones. $110.00. Right: Gold, topaz, and lime green rhinestone brooch and earrings. $155.00.

Left: Diamente rhinestone brooch. $110.00. Right: Diamente rhinestone brooch and earrings. $165.00.

Top: Pink and blue rhinestone brooch has aurora borealis rhinestones also. $95.00. Right: "Diamond Look" diamente rhinestones. Two layers of three petals each in brooch, earrings have just one petal each. $295.00.

Left: Citrine and gold navette rhinestone brooch and earrings. $160.00. Right: Gold, topaz, and aurora borealis rhinestone brooch and earrings. $180.00.

Top: Explosion of gold-plated cones has diamente rhinestones. Brooch and earrings. $165.00. Middle: Golden pear brooch and earrings. Pavé diamente rhinestones. $140.00. Right: Gold-plated blossom brooch and earrings, pavé diamente rhinestones. $110.00.

Black net over smoky rhinestone brooch and earrings. $180.00.

Left: Pink, fuchsia, and aurora borealis rhinestones. Three-dimensional brooch and earrings. $280.00. Right: Opalene cabochons, aurora borealis rhinestones in brooch and earrings. $150.00.

211

Clockwise from top left: Gold-plated brooch, ribs of pavé diamente rhinestones. $55.00. Twisted gold-plated twin ropes brooch. $55.00. Gold-plated heart has blue rhinestones. $75.00. Earrings match twin ropes brooch. $45.00.

Top: Montana blue cabochons and clear rhinestone brooch. $60.00. Left: Light blue and lavender horseshoe rhinestone brooch. $110.00. Right: Rectangular brooch uses two shades of blue rhinestones. $80.00.

Top: Teal blue and diamente rhinestone domed brooch. $75.00. Bottom: Diamente navette rhinestones tipped with sapphire blue rhinestones. Brooch. $80.00.

Top: Japanned brooch with clear diamente rhinestones. $58.00. Right: Four blossoms, gold-plated, clear rhinestones. $95.00. Bottom: Dentelle center, aurora borealis and diamente rhinestone brooch. $125.00.

Left: Brooch with various sizes of diamente rhinestones and pearls. $235.00. Right: Diamente rhinestone brooch. $125.00.

Left: Rows of citrine and gold rhinestones. Brooch. $155.00. Right: Japanned, two shades of blue rhinestones. Brooch. $85.00.

Top: Pearl and diamente rhinestone wheel brooch. $80.00. Bottom: Diamente and blue rhinestone wheel brooch. $105.00.

Top: Two shades of green rhinestones. Snowflake design brooch. $85.00. Left: Mint green glass stones. Brooch. $58.00. Right: Floral spray brooch, green glass, pearls, and green rhinestones. $72.00.

Left: Gold-plated flower, blue rhinestones. $55.00. Top: Imitation lapis cabochon brooch. $65.00. Bottom: Imitation jade cabochon brooch. $78.00.

213

Left: Gold-plated crown with crystals. $165.00.
Right: Scepter and crown brooch. Clear, blue, and
red rhinestones. $185.00.

Left: Rose with enamel leaves and gold rhinestones.
$78.00. Right: Enamel rose brooch and earrings.
$95.00.

Top: Bird brooch with seed pearl
body. $58.00. Middle: Diamente
rhinestone bird. $160.00. Bottom:
Opalene bird earrings. $75.00.

Left: Gold-plated butterfly with diamente rhinestones.
$78.00. Top: Shades of blue and green rhinestone but-
terfly. $155.00. Bottom: Gold-plated horse, diamente
rhinestone trim, chain tassel tail. $90.00.

Enamel bird on branch with nest of pearls. $180.00.

Left: Enamel bee, green rhinestone eyes. $95.00. Right: Enamel insect, pavé diamente upper wing. $95.00. Bottom: Blue faceted crystal stone and pavé diamente rhinestone turtle. $80.00.

Top: Can can girl, pearl skirt and head, diamente rhinestone accents. $145.00. Bottom: Gold-plated articulated bracelet, clear rhinestones. $80.00.

215

Enamel Santa Claus, diamente
rhinestone face. $125.00.

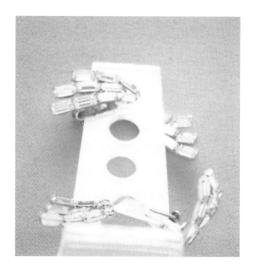

Front and back of diamente rhinestone
earrings. Fashioned to glitter both from
in front of and behind the ear lobe.

Eight pairs of earrings. $40.00 – 65.00.

Front and back of diamente rhinestone ear covers.
Curved wire hoop fits over top of ear.

Mazer Brothers

History

Began: 1927
Closed: 1970
Designers: Joseph Mazer
Lincoln Mazer
Signed: Mazer 1927 – 1970
Jomaz 1950 – 1970
Joseph Mazer 1950 – 1970

Characteristics

Look of fine jewelry
Skilled use of plastics
Mass production
Wide range of styles
Mid-price market

The Mazer family left their native Russia in the mid-1920s. Their country was torn by civil warfare, and Samuel Mazer brought his seven young sons to the land of promise, America.

Brothers Joseph, Abe, and Harry hand-set rhinestones at the Franco American Bead Company in Philadelphia and began learning about the American business world.

The young brothers, Joseph and Lincoln, lost no time in starting their own shoe buckle business. Their highly decorative buckles caught the eye of fashion jewelry designer Marcel Boucher, and he encouraged the Mazer Brothers Company to venture into the costume jewelry world in 1927.

Samuel Mazer helped develop synthetic rubber, and the Mazer Brothers did the engraving work for Catalin Company Plastics. The brothers designed jewelry for the mid-price market and covered a wide range of style in mass production.

From 1927 to 1950, the brothers combined their efforts in the business. In 1950, the brothers separated. Joseph named his company the Joseph J. Mazer & Co., Inc. He used the trademarks Jomaz and Joseph Mazer after that date.

Brother Lincoln established the Mazer Company, also known for their high standards. Both firms continued the Mazer reputation of quality and beauty until 1970.

Diamente rhinestone baguettes with sapphire blue rhinestones in necklace and earrings. $145.00.

Top: Gold-plated, clear rhinestones and pearls brooch. $90.00. Bottom: Gold-plated clear rhinestones and pink crystal earrings. $65.00.

Purple cabochons, pink glass stones necklace and earrings. $375.00.

Left: Matte gold finish, clear rhinestone flower clusters brooch and earrings. $180.00. Right: Gold swirl, rows of diamente rhinestone brooch and earrings. $195.00.

Crown brooch and earrings. Clear, red, green, and blue rhinestones. $250.00.

218

Fur clip and earrings feature emerald green and clear rhinestones. Dark green crystal drop. $225.00.

Left: Art Nouveau imitation turquoise and enameling brooch and earrings. $175.00. Right: Gold-plated seed pod filled with blue and clear rhinestones. Brooch and earrings. $210.00.

Imitation emerald parure of ring, necklace, earrings, and bracelet. Clear rhinestone accents. $550.00.

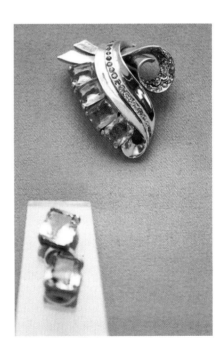

Gold-plated fur clip and earrings. Aquamarine crystals. $280.00.

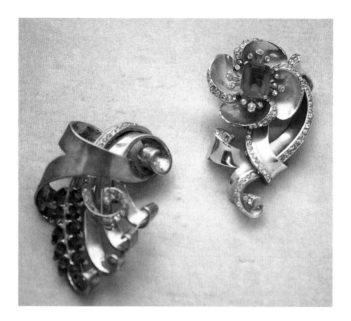

Left: Gold-plated red rhinestone fur clip. $250.00. Right: Gold-plated flower fur clip. Large red crystal and pavé diamente rhinestones. $250.00.

Ruby and pink crystal stones, pavé diamente brooch. $295.00.

Red, clear, and blue rhinestone floral brooch. $190.00.

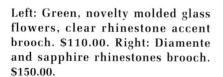

Left: Green, novelty molded glass flowers, clear rhinestone accent brooch. $110.00. Right: Diamente and sapphire rhinestones brooch. $150.00.

Left: Gold-plated and diamente rhinestone brooch. $110.00. Right: Dark green cabochon, diamente rhinestone brooch. $150.00.

Top: Pavé flower petals of pink rhinestones, purple rhinestone cluster center. $90.00. Bottom: Gold-plated brooch, blue cabochons, pavé diamente rhinestone center. $75.00.

Top: Fur clip with emerald cut topaz, trimmed in pavé diamente rhinestones. $195.00. Bottom: Brooch with large turquoise cabochon, pavé diamente rhinestones. $110.00.

Left: Lavender and amethyst cabochon necklace. $110.00. Right: Enamel floral necklace. $80.00.

Left: Imitation jade cabochon belly. Pavé diamente rhinestone bear. $95.00. Middle: Turquoise belly squirrel, dark green rhinestone eyes, pavé diamente rhinestone tail. $105.00. Right: Roadrunner. $80.00.

Left: Imitation emerald earrings and bracelet. Diamente rhinestones. $150.00. Right: Imitation ruby bracelet, diamente rhinestones. $98.00.

Left: Male lion, diamente rhinestone checks and eyes. $125.00. Right: Long-eared dog. $80.00.

Top: Buck-toothed rabbit. $80.00. Bottom: Skiing rabbit, pearl bunny tail. $85.00.

Enamel pin-tail duck, clear rhinestones. $225.00.

Left: Diamond rhinestone floral brooch. $135.00.
Right: Diamond rhinestone long-stemmed flower.
$155.00.

Left: Gold-plated umbrella, basket of pearls and
clear rhinestones. $135.00. Top: Gold-plated
diamente rhinestone bird on twig. $75.00. Bot-
tom: Imitation jade statue brooch. $135.00.

Enamel peacock, blue, green, and
clear rhinestones. $200.00.

Left: Imitation jade cabochon, diamente rhinestones.
$145.00. Right: Imitation jade belly seahorse. Blue
enamel mane, diamente rhinestone cheeks. $95.00.

Metalcraft

The sparkle of rhinestones drew many of us into admiring and collecting at the beginning. And after examining each newly found treasure, we have become aware of the jeweler's craft and skill.

The veins in a leaf, the curly wisp of hair on a forehead, the folds of a gown are minute details that add to the overall beauty of this American art form.

Examine the work of this man, a metalcraft genius, closely, and then begin to watch for it when you are shopping.

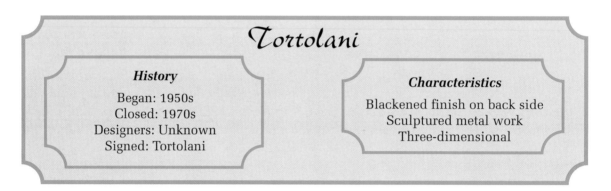

Tortolani

History

Began: 1950s
Closed: 1970s
Designers: Unknown
Signed: Tortolani

Characteristics

Blackened finish on back side
Sculptured metal work
Three-dimensional

As I became more and more immersed in the American costume jewelry art form, the quality and skill of the artisans began to draw me as much as the colorful rhinestones.

I first became acquainted with the Tortolani company when I picked up an angel thinking it was a Christmas holiday brooch. It fascinated me with the clever design that allowed the brooch to sit on the shoulder. The designer had managed to translate from the drawing board the personality that was now in the sparkling blue eyes. But the best was yet to come; the clerk said, "Please look at the other one." There was a matching devil. The legend is that you put an angel on one shoulder and the devil on the other to allow you to send signals of your mood when out with your significant other. See these brooches at the top of page 227.

Research uncovered that Tortolani was in production from the 1950s into the 1970s. They specialized in antique silver and gold-plated finishes. Concentrating on the sculpturing of the metal, they depended on the design to carry the strength of the jewelry, using rhinestones and faux pearls very sparingly. Their work frequently became three-dimensional with ample area for fully detailing every feature.

If you will turn over a piece of their work, you will immediately notice an antique finish that blackens the back of the jewelry. This is an important clue when trying to identify who made the piece as you are shopping. Of course, there is a cartouche bearing the company name, Tortolani, but you need a loupe or magnifying glass to read it.

Careful attention has been given to facial details in all the figural designs. Even the hair has been combed to eternal perfection. Whatever the sport they are participating in, bowling, golf, baseball or just clowning around, Tortolani has given them all a personality. The fascinating question in my mind is how did he incorporate such warmth in cold metal?

The same attention to detail has been extended to all his productions. On several of the pieces I have located two cartouches. Many times, a shopper has been disappointed because costume jewelry is unmarked, but Tortolani was so careful to identify his work that you can find some pieces that have been marked twice.

Antique gold rose parure of necklace, brooch, and earrings. $450.00.

Antique pewter finish zodiac earrings, necklace, and bracelet. $1,100.00.

Faux pearl necklace and earrings. $110.00.

Desert theme collar necklace and earrings. $125.00.

Antique pewter finish necklace and two styles of earrings. $105.00.

Zodiac signs necklace, brooch, and ring. $150.00

Left: Articulated sea horse pendant. $95.00. Right: Turtle necklace. $150.00.

Devil and angel brooches. $225.00.

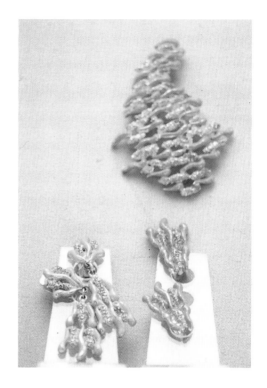

Top and bottom right: Enameled coral brooch and earrings with sea kelp. $80.00. Bottom left: Coral and sea kelp dangle earrings. $45.00.

Top left: Faux pearl brooch. $56.00. Top right and bottom: Faux pearl flower brooch and earrings. $85.00.

Top left: Faux pearl, silver-plated brooch. $70.00. Top right and bottom: Same brooch design in gold plating with earrings. $95.00.

Top: Art Deco birds, pink and green crushed stone. $110.00. Bottom: Bonsai tree, silver-plated. $195.00.

Top: Gold-plated fireworks plume. $65.00. Left: Gold-plated ribbon circle. $70.00. Right: Silver-plated leaves. $48.00.

Left: Gold-plated dancer. $85.00. Right: Enameled dancer. $98.00.

Sports figures. $55.00 – 78.00. Center: Ballerina. $85.00.

Left: Enamel pixie on a crescent moon. $175.00. Right: Silver-plated fairy. $150.00.

228

Left: Cherub. $78.00. Middle: Scarecrow. $65.00. Right: Market Street trolley. $125.00.

Top: Faux pearl, gold-plated bird on branch. $80.00. Bottom: Roadrunner. $90.00.

Left: Imitation jade cabochon swan. $140.00. Right: Enamel flower. $80.00.

Left: Gold-plated elephant. $95.00. Right: Elephant pill box. $145.00.

Unattributed Designs

Information is not readily available on many of the jewelry industry companies. The 1970s tolled the death knell for many, and their businesses have been closed for over 30 years.

The people who were involved in their operations have retired, moved or died. Company records were trashed, archives bought up by strangers, and factories renovated, but their jewelry lives on.

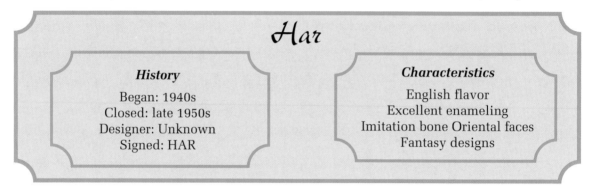

Har

History

Began: 1940s
Closed: late 1950s
Designer: Unknown
Signed: HAR

Characteristics

English flavor
Excellent enameling
Imitation bone Oriental faces
Fantasy designs

And then there is the mystery company with the overseas connection, entwined with the ticking of Old Ben and the London fog rolling in. During the 1940s there was a firm who signed all their jewelry, HAR. For almost 20 years their designers turned out charming pieces that not only had an English touch but jewelry that had a continental air, from the wide expanse of the British Empire.

One fable has been told that an English immigrant started up the business located in the Boston area but became so homesick that he just locked the doors and went back to England. If that is so, it was certainly our misfortune to lose such talent.

I have to admit my lack of knowledge about the history of this firm, but I would be remiss if I deprived you of meeting Har through their great jewelry designs.

Prepare yourself for the treat of a lifetime, at least for a jewelry collector. Here comes the parade of dragons, genies, and smiling Chinese.

Our genie is 2⅜" tall and 2" wide (see top of next page.) He has a deep bronze skin tone. The waist-high figural wearing gold arm bands has a gold vest with diamente ribbon trim. His sapphire studded turban has a red cabochon, and his crystal ball has a golden star with a blue rhinestone center. But Har did not stop there — look at the matching earrings. They are the turbaned genie complete with crystal ball.

You'll meet the genie again on the magical bracelet (see bottom of next page). Chest-high, he is the spitting image of the brooch. Seven inches long,

the bracelet's four main links are 1¼" squares. Aladdin's magic lamp has a crystal pot with a plume of smoke curling up. Another link is the sultan's castle, and the magic looking glass ball becomes the fourth link. The full-figure genie can be seen balancing a tray holding the magic looking glass.

From the mystic world of India, Har goes to ancient China for the mythical dragon (see page 232). The full body of the dragon wraps around the wrist with listening ears and darting tongue. He has dark green scales and is adorned with aurora borealis rhinestones and stones that simulate molten lava. The coiled dragon becomes a pin, but the most adorable are the miniature dragon earrings.

The circa 1955 parure (top left, page 233) consisting of two brooches, earrings, and charm bracelet feature the smiling Oriental faces of imitation bone, also called the "Happy Asian." The 14" brooch's figure shows the coolie's hand and robe to the waist, done in antique gold finish. The 1½" tall brooch uses the Oriental face but has just a golden collar studded with imitation green cabochons and aurora borealis rhinestones. Earring faces do not have the hat on the 1½" clip-backs. The 8" chain bracelet has one smiling face charm.

Oh, look, here he is again, but this brooch and earring set has been done in white enamel with hand brushed touches of gold (bottom right, page 232). Which effect do you like best? I just had to have both.

Looking at all this outstanding Har jewelry, don't you feel you now know the company?

Genie brooch and earrings. $450.00.

Left: Turbaned regal African. $225.00. Right: Full-figure genie. $340.00.

Genie bracelet. $1,150.00.

Dragon bracelet.

Dragon brooch.

Dragon earrings. Four-piece parure, $1,950.00.

Smiling Chinese coolie brooch and earrings. $525.00.

Smiling Chinese coolie parure.
$1,400.00.

Left: Imitation jade and faux pearl parure of brooch, bracelet, and earrings. $125.00. Right: Brooch, bracelet, and earrings parure. Bronze and teal buds, navette aurora borealis, and topaz rhinestones. $250.00.

Left: 3¼" x 3" brooch with 1⅜" faceted amethyst glass stone. Picture frame with seed pearls setting. Matching earrings. $120.00. Right: Flower head brooch, red rhinestone center, antique gold finish. Matching earrings. $95.00.

Left: Art Deco brooch with 1½" topaz glass stone. Japanned fittings have tripod-shaped rhinestones. Matching earrings. $150.00. Right: Antique gold oval brooch and earrings. Two rows of gold ribbon candy, olive green rhinestones. $90.00.

233

Left: Enameled pear with pavé rhinestone leaf. $60.00.
Right: Enameled cherries on branch, pavé leaf. $75.00.

Top: Aurora borealis pear-shaped rhinestones form six points. $45.00. Middle: Double twisted gold braid ropes interspersed with imitation lapis beads. $60.00. Bottom: Imitation red coral beads, seed pearls. $35.00.

Top: Gold-plated leaves with lapis beads and pearls. $45.00. Left: Faux pearl, aurora borealis rhinestones swirl. $55.00. Right: Matte gold finish, small pearls, double tiered, pavé center. $50.00.

Top: Enamel star, ruby center rimmed with small blue rhinestones. $45.00. Right: Pineapple, turquoise beads. $30.00. Left: Seed pearl flowers, gold-plated brooch. $35.00.

234

Top: Gold bug, pavé body, green rhinestone eyes. $60.00. Middle: Gold-plated insect, turquoise beads. $55.00. Bottom: Green enamel four-leaf clover, topaz cabochons. $38.00.

Left: Enamel organ grinder monkey. $65.00. Middle: English bobbie, enameled. $90.00. Right: Enamel dog, pink beret. $40.00.

Top left: Fish, gold-plated tassel fins, tail and head. Boyd glass orange and black stone. $60.00. Top right: Enamel leaf, blue caterpillar. $75.00. Bottom: Black enameled lizard, red rhinestones. $75.00.

Clockwise from top left: Red glass cabochon turtle. $45.00. Turtle with green enamel head and feet. Red cabochon body has gold lattice work. $70.00. Imitation turquoise cabochon turtle. $55.00. Enamel turtle, white shell, pink ribbon. $65.00.

Left: Enamel mouse, pink ears, cheeks, and bow. $75.00. Right: Enamel cat, green rhinestone eyes, blue ball of yarn (glass stone). $60.00.

Three enamel figures. $48.00 each.

Top: Royal scepter with double chain, wrapped pavé ribbon and faux pearls. $115.00. Bottom: Faux turquoise glass beads and cabochon, pearl turtle. $54.00.

Left: Bird with red head and tail feathers, pearl body. $65.00. Right: Enamel penguin with red turtle-necked sweater and knitted cap. $95.00.

Top: Art Deco enameled bug. $48.00. Left: Art Deco enameled flower. $55.00. Right: Enamel flower, milk white beads. $35.00.

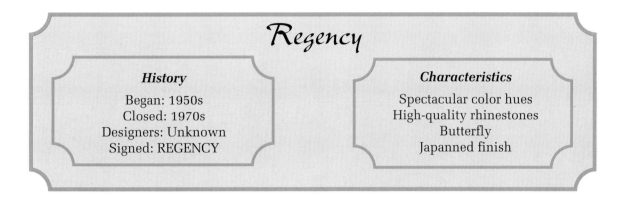

Regency

History

Began: 1950s
Closed: 1970s
Designers: Unknown
Signed: REGENCY

Characteristics

Spectacular color hues
High-quality rhinestones
Butterfly
Japanned finish

I've always liked a good detective story. My only regret is that I have several unsolved mysteries on my mind, and I have yet to meet Sherlock Holmes.

This company, with the most spectacular colors of rhinestones, proudly marked their pieces "REGENCY," always in capital letters, but the firm left little information about the business.

The jewelry is believed to have been produced by the Regent Jewelry Company, located at Number 20, either on 36th or 37th Street, deep in the heart of the jewelry district of New York City, and in business during the 1950s, closing its doors in the 1970s.

From the style of the designs, it has been established that the jewelry is indeed from that time period. Look carefully at the Regency picture section and feast your eyes on the richness of the colors. You will never see one of their stones that is not filled to the brim with a depth of hue that is almost blinding. Their beauty is eternal.

This company used a coal tar derivative to plate the brooches in the black finish called japanning. This black finish sets off the darker hued rhinestones.

Every company usually included butterflies in their line, but no one made them like Regency. When my childern were tiny, they called them "flutterbys," and Regency's certainly do just that. Examine the creatures on page 241, and I know you will agree with me.

In the picture at bottom left of page 240, you can quickly see what the correct colored rhinestones can do for a fitting. These 4" brooches use the same fitting but are dressed differently. The gold-plated version features gold, orange, and lime green rhinestones in navette, teardrop, and chaton shapes. The second version is japanned with light and dark green shades of rhinestones.

Their wholesale line was sold directly to leading department stores in New York, Chicago, and other larger cities. Morty Polowitz, son of the owner, went to sunny California when the firm shut down and was a jewelry line representative until about 10 years ago.

But then the trail grows cold, and even AT&T cannot find a telephone listing in the entire state of California. Morty Polowitz, where are you? Morty, if you are out there, please contact me. I want to thank you and your father for all the beautiful treasures your family created.

Parure consisting of necklace, earrings, brooch, and bracelet. Pink, red, and aurora borealis rhinestones. $275.00.

Olive green and aurora borealis rhinestone parure of brooch, earrings, and necklace. $195.00 – 210.00.

Light blue cabochons, gold and blue rhinestone parure of bracelet, brooch, and earrings. $200.00.

Japanned designs featuring diamente and smoky rhinestones. Left: Necklace. $90.00. Top: Star shaped-brooch. $84.00. Bottom: Snowflake brooch. $90.00.

Japanned leaf brooch and earrings. Three shades of green and aurora borealis rhinestones. $135.00.

Left: Topaz faceted glass center stone brooch and earrings. Aurora borealis, citrine rhinestones. $132.00. Right: Two shades of blue rhinestone brooch and earrings. $110.00.

Clockwise from top: Trapezoidal brown and gold stones in brooch with topaz and green rhinestones. $110.00. Brooch with twin blossoms of topaz, lime green, and aurora borealis rhinestones. $80.00. Clip-on earrings in fall colors. $38.00. Japanned flower with aurora borealis and topaz rhinestones. $95.00.

Left: Citrine and aurora borealis brooch. $110.00. Right: Citrine and aurora borealis snowflake brooch and earrings. $130.00.

Left: Pearl, gold leaves, and diamente rhinestone brooch and earrings. $145.00. Right: Japanned brooch and earrings. Teal and dark blue rhinestones. $190.00.

Left: Purple and fuchsia rhinestone brooch and earrings. $155.00. Right: Similar design brooch and earrings in pink and aurora borealis rhinestones. $130.00.

Left: Opaque cabochon and drop brooch with citrine and topaz rhinestones. $160.00. Right: Fall brooch and earrings with topaz, brown, and aurora borealis rhinestones. $140.00.

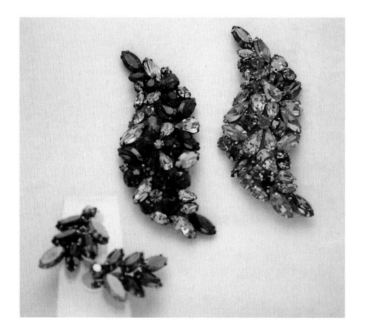

Left: Earrings and brooch in three shades of green rhinestones. $160.00. Right: Same design brooch dressed in shades of orange and green rhinestones. $110.00.

Left: 1¾" silver-plated butterfly with shades of blue rhinestones. $85.00. Right: 2¾" butterfly and earrings in shades of blue rhinestones, silver-plated. $140.00.

Left: 1¾" butterfly and earrings in shades of green rhinestones. $105.00. Right: 2¾" orange and topaz rhinestone butterfly and earrings. $155.00.

Top: 1½" red rhinestone, gold-plated butterfly. $85.00. Bottom: Japanned butterfly and earrings have faux turquoise and white chalk navette stones. Topaz, green, and citrine rhinestones. $180.00.

Top: Red rhinestone butterfly in flight. $85.00. Left: Pink rhinestone butterfly in flight with earrings. $135.00. Right: Blue and green rhinestone butterfly in flight. $90.00.

Top: Novelty glass body bug with pink and aurora borealis rhinestones. $75.00. Bottom: Lime green butterfly. $105.00. Right: Pair of bugs. $45.00 – 55.00 each.

241

Four rows of aurora borealis rhinestone brooch. $135.00.

Clockwise from top: Crackle and lemon glass cabochons with aurora
borealis rhinestone brooch. $80.00. Pink and yellow-green rhinestone
brooch. $90.00. Aurora borealis rhinestones, japanned finish. $95.00.
Light and dark green rhinestone brooch. $98.00.

Top: Blue bead, blue and aurora
borealis rhinestone brooch.
$90.00. Bottom: Three-leaf clover
brooch. Turquoise with shades of
blue rhinestones. $68.00

Purple, aurora borealis, and
clear rhinestone brooch.
$180.00.

242

Top: Maltese cross in blue and lime green rhinestones. $80.00. Bottom: Maltese cross in multicolored rhinestones. $95.00.

Top left: Blue glass cabochon, blue rhinestone brooch. $73.00. Top right: Faux pearl, blue rhinestone brooch. $92.00. Bottom: Blue crystal and blue rhinestone brooch. $110.00.

Top: Gold-plated crown with aurora borealis and gold rhinestones. $115.00. Bottom: Orange, topaz, aurora borealis rhinestone brooch. $95.00. Right: Imitation tiger eye cabochons, amber and aurora borealis rhinestone bracelet. $78.00.

Left: Three row bracelet of light and dark blue rhinestones. $85.00. Right: Lime green crystals, green and aurora borealis rhinestones. $110.00.

Women of Distinction

Numerous women made their marks in the history of the jewelry industry, and I have selected four to highlight here, women whom I have grown to admire for their creations and business integrity.

These are women who are to be admired for their dedication to the beautification of all women and for their commitment to the preservation of the American art form of costume jewelry.

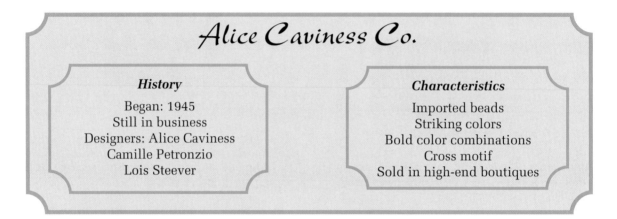

Alice Caviness Co.

History

Began: 1945
Still in business
Designers: Alice Caviness
Camille Petronzio
Lois Steever

Characteristics

Imported beads
Striking colors
Bold color combinations
Cross motif
Sold in high-end boutiques

The legacy of Alice Caviness is in the bold, imaginative colors of costume jewelry that truly reveal the personality and character of the woman behind the sparkling rhinestone reflections and flowing design lines of each piece bearing her name.

A raised oval tag with Alice Caviness emblazoned in block letters soldered on the back of her jewelry proudly proclaims the reason that buyers eagerly add her jewelry to their collections.

This woman of style without compromise, who was the epitome of the woman of the 1990s, was actually a business woman of the 1940s.

Alice Caviness opened her jewelry business in 1945, combining her flair for style with her husband's astute salesmanship. They were very fortunate in their close association with Jack Li Buno, owner of Jacques Jewelry. He was able to take their ideas and create masterpieces in sterling, vermeils, enamels, pearls, and gold.

In close partnership with her husband, Mr. Junquera, she made many business trips to Europe to purchase fine beads, pearls, and other findings. She charmed the French with her style and mode of dress. Her costumes were completed with her personal jewelry that brought raves from the fashion houses. Soon her foreign trips were not buying expeditions but selling excursions as the Europeans began buying her line for their specialty boutiques.

Not only did Alice design her own jewelry line, but she was involved in every step of design, production, and sales. From beginning to end she was personally responsible for each piece of jewelry bearing her name. She had the imagination to envision a dream and the ability to see it through. When she wanted a large factory to produce her jewelry, she worked hand-in-hand with her plant manager in drawing out the floor plan to make sure that quality was uppermost at every stage of production.

Alice was even very careful to select shops that would reflect her good taste. Her jewelry could only be found in high-end boutique shops where shoppers with money could find her beautiful line to lend the finishing touch on their costumes.

Estee Lauder soon heard of this marvelous woman and her jewelry. Ms. Lauder expressed an interest in a merger with Caviness. Caviness, the independent woman, would not relinquish her hands-on business technique and opted to continue to do things her way.

Little escaped her as the head of her own business, and she shared her knowledge generously. Designers Camille Petronzio and Lois Steever can testify to her astuteness in recognizing and developing their potential.

They both came to the Caviness operation fresh out of high school. No restraints were placed on their learning the business; instead, the two young girls were cultivated and their talents developed.

Beginning as a shipping clerk, Camille became a designer of three collections a year for Caviness. Now she is the head designer for Miriam Haskell. Lois was originally a secretary and became a designer after five years in the company. In 1980 Lois became president of the Alice Caviness Company.

Failing health dimmed her eyes, and Alice retired from active jewelry work in 1970. She died in 1983, but her legacy lives on in the fine jewelry proudly worn by today's collectors.

Silver-plated parure of necklace, brooch, and earrings. Imitation diamond chaton, navette rhinestones. $195.00.

Gold-plated parure of necklace, brooch, and earrings. Aurora borealis chaton rhinestones; pink navette rhinestones add color. $250.00.

Summer pink parure of necklace, bracelet, and earrings. Four-strand necklace has pink beads, pearls, and gold spacers. Same bead work in three-strand bracelet. $165.00.

Two strands of necklace are formed by alternate links of clear and red rhinestones connecting three high-domed red cabochons. All three are framed by clear and red rhinestones. Matching earrings. $350.00.

Gold-plated necklace and earrings. Triple strand, draped clear rhinestone chain. Six gold medallion accents have pavé diamente centers. Matching earrings. $275.00.

Pink necklace of faceted glass and pink milk glass beads with a suspended pink enamel ball encrusted with pink rhinestones. Earrings have pink beads. $195.00.

Filigree necklace and bracelet. Each link has gold rhinestone centers. $140.00.

Ankh necklace decorated with fall shade rhinestones and cabochons. Matching earrings. $350.00.

Imitation bone slices and aurora borealis and gold beads used in necklace and earrings. Three-strand necklace. $110.00.

Six-strand gold-plated necklace with a center of pearls, rhinestones, and colored glass beads. Tassel endings have the same ornamentation. Gold floral findings top larger beads. $125.00.

Top: Egyptian-style gold-plated collar necklace with two decorative rows of golden circles filled with red rhinestones. $110.00. Bottom: Gold-plated cat with red rhinestone body. $50.00.

Pink chalk beads fill out decorative circle of double chained necklace. Matching earrings. $125.00.

White and blue satin bead necklace with small clear, blue rhinestone, and white enamel filigree balls. $75.00. Center: Blue frosted rhinestone brooch. $80.00.

Left: Oriental imitation jade molded brooch with bamboo frame. $65.00. Right: Oriental imitation coral molded pendant on antique gold-plated chain has bamboo frame with three suspended Chinese symbols. $110.00.

Enamel owl with cabochon eyes hangs from necklace. $80.00. Bottom: Pink and blue rhinestone butterfly brooch is framed with twisted gold chain. $95.00.

Left: Brown tone glass cabochons and aurora borealis rhinestone brooch and earrings. $95.00. Right: Opalescent glass stones used with gold and clear rhinestones in brooch. $125.00.

Left: Lavender glass cabochons with aurora borealis rhinestones of various shapes in brooch and matching earrings. $135.00. Right: Gold metallic rhinestones are enhanced by gold-colored rhinestones in brooch and earrings. $150.00.

Blue toned plastic brooch and earrings. $110.00.

Left: Coral-colored navette feather brooch and earrings. $85.00. Right: Dog-toothed pink moonstone cabochons and light green rhinestones in brooch and earrings. $125.00.

Sterling silver. Top left: Filigree butterfly. $165.00. Top right: Flower with filigree leaves. $130.00. Bottom: Leaf and earrings have flower motif. $155.00.

Clockwise from top left: Clear and aurora borealis navette rhinestone brooch. $75.00. Gold metallic and aurora borealis navette rhinestone brooch. $95.00. Blue and aurora borealis navette and chaton rhinestone brooch. $130.00.

Brooch, 2", faceted amber-colored, center stone framed with aurora borealis rhinestones. $350.00.

Clockwise from left: Lavender rhinestones with three amethyst drops. $150.00. Lime green and aurora borealis with gold glass droplets. $95.00. Clear ornament has a swirl of white cloud nestled in mint green navette rhinestones. $195.00.

Top: Amber-colored rhinestone brooch. $105.00. Right: Imitation onyx banjo with clear rhinestone outlining. $95.00. Bottom: Gold-plated clear rhinestone earrings. $30.00.

Left: Brooch utilizing pearls and aurora borealis rhinestones of various sizes. $65.00. Bottom: Gold-plated brooch with large light yellow rhinestones. $40.00. Right: Opalene drops and cabochon with gold chain and aurora borealis rhinestones brooch. $145.00.

Clockwise from left: Imitation turquoise body butterfly with wings of light blue and green rhinestones. $80.00. Pink, lavender, and fuchsia butterfly, gold-plated. $135.00. Blue and clear rhinestone navettes combined with light green navette cabochons brooch. $80.00. Insect with enamel wings, lavender cabochon body, lavender rhinestone head. $65.00.

Left: Gold-plated pineapple. $55.00. Top: Pearl studded gold-plated pineapple. $70.00. Bottom: Pair of gold-plated pineapple brooches. $85.00.

Top: Japanned finish, blue tone rhinestone butterfly. $165.00. Bottom left: Japanned finish, blue toned swordfish. $145.00. Bottom right: Matching butterfly earrings. $35.00.

Left: Citrine to cocoa rhinestone butterfly. $150.00. Right: Cocoa and yellow rhinestone butterfly. $95.00.

Left: Silver-plated, lavender cabochon and aurora borealis rhinestone bracelet. $85.00. Right: Citrine and clear rhinestone link bracelet. $65.00.

Left: Aurora borealis earrings and matching bracelet. $145.00. Right: Shades of green and aurora borealis rhinestone bracelet. $68.00.

Cuff bracelet utilizes pearls, rhinestones, and soft blue glass stones of various sizes and shapes. $285.00.

Mimi di N

History

Began: 1960
Still in business
Designer: Mimi di Niscemi
Signed: Mimi di N

Characteristics

Manipulated pieces
Dramatic and bold
Elaborate jewelry
Byzantine style

Mimi di Niscemi was born in Palermo, Sicily, spent part of her childhood there and part in Philadelphia, Pennsylvania. Her family lineage included a cousin, the internationally famous Fulco di Verduor, a well-known European jewelry and fashion designer. It was no wonder that she also inherited artistic talents.

Those talents must have guided her to choose to study at the Philadelphia Museum School of Industrial Arts, a fortunate choice since it allowed her to work part-time at a jewelry manufacturer who produced Schiaparelli jewelry. There she had hands-on training and learned the art of manipulation of metal.

Her skills soon drew the attention of the Dutch silversmith Rudolph Broom, and she began working with him at the Wichita Art Association. Her extensive background and talent earned her a scholarship to the School of Applied Arts in Paris. She became proficient in goldsmithing, silversmithing, wrought iron, metal working and rendering, skills that would serve her well in the jewelry world.

It did not take long for her to win recognition as a highly talented designer, and she was offered a partnership with the clothing designer Arnold Scaasi. The costume jewelry division, formed in the 1950s, produced pieces marked "Jewels by Scaasi."

In 1959 she joined Robert De Mario, applying all the skills she had learned both here and in Europe. She soon moved on to the famous New York bead house Brania where she made show-stopping, runway jewels marked "Brania/Mimi di N."

All her hard work gave her confidence and built a reputation that enabled her to venture out, opening her own jewelry firm in New York City in 1960. The name "Mimi di N" can be found in dramatic, bold, elaborate, manipulated pieces. Her style was influenced by her Sicilian heritage and her new association with the Russian heritage after she married the grand nephew of Czar Nicolas II, Prince Alexander Romanoff.

Her treasury of jewelry is a library of timeless designs that are truly gems to be catalogued, inventoried, and protected.

Eight-strand torsade of lavender and green glass tube beads, rhinestone rondels. $300.00.

4" Art Deco gold-plated brooch. Faux pearl center, scattered diamente rhinestones. $250.00.

Gold-plated linked rings necklace supports 3" gold-plated frog with imitation jade green eyes. $350.00.

Clear crystal petal flower with rhinestone center. $195.00.

Enamel turtle, faux turquoise cabochon, gold-plated, green rhinestone eyes. $145.00.

Winking owl, gold-plated. Open eye is red bead. $110.00.

Nettie Rosenstein

History

Began: 1948
Closed: 1970
Designer: Nettie Rosenstein
Signed: Nettie Rosenstein

Characteristics

Limited availability
Buy when you find it
Distinctive
Stylish

Nettie Rosenstein was born in Vienna, Austria, in 1890, and came to the United States at the tender age of two. Her family name was changed to Rosenstein when they settled in New York.

Her early childhood was uneventful as the twentieth century approached. As were most young girls of that historical period, she was a gifted seamstress.

It was very socially acceptable for a young woman of good manners and breeding to enter the garment industry. Nettie and her older sister decided to start a millinery business. Their fine work soon attracted many clients.

In fact, by the year 1921, there were 50 seamstresses employed to turn out her clothing designs as Nettie used her talents to expand the business.

Her beautiful lingerie was only a part of her business that was devoted to the feminine mystique. She truly catered to the complete woman, offering custom perfume and body soap as the starting touch for the well-dressed woman.

At the height of her success, Nettie chose to retire from the fashion world. Her clientele sorely missed her and let it be known that her disappearance was a blow to the New York fashion scene.

She made a triumphant return to New York in 1932 when she opened her 7th Avenue house of couture. She reigned for almost 30 years, giving the fashion world such famous trademarks as "the little black dress."

At the age of 70, her clothing line was discontinued, and she concentrated on her accessory lines which included costume jewelry, perfume, and handbags.

Presentation of her line was always important to her. Jewelry was offered in small black velvet drawstring bags that were lined in gold-colored satin and bore the name "Nettie Rosenstein." One side of the bag had a compartment for the brooch, and the other side had a split compartment for the pair of earrings. An impressive finishing touch to her beautiful jewelry.

Nettie Rosenstein continued to put the finishing touches on the fashionable women of the world until 1970 when she closed the doors of her company. Nettie died at the age of 90 in 1980. The 50 whirlwind years she was in business were just a brief passage of time, but she will long be remembered.

Hollow, gold-plated, pitted strawberry brooch, 2½" x 1¾", and earrings. Black drawstring bag. $350.00.

White enamel outline flower, red and clear rhinestone center. $135.00.

Left: Gold carnations. $85.00. Right: Gold-plated pansy earrings, blue cabochons, pavé diamente rhinestones in center. $75.00.

Sterling silver fur clip with hanging double chain, tassel ends. Scepter has large, faceted emerald green chaton trimmed with seed pearls. $340.00.

Red enamel apple fur clip. Green enamel leaves have ribs of pink vermeil. $165.00.

Sterling silver 2½" butterfly, enamel wings, Peking glass cabochons, clear rhinestones. $140.00.

Adele Simpson

History

Began: 1930s
Closed: Unknown
Designers: Adele Simpson
Henry Schreiner
Signed: Adele Simpson

Characteristics

Limited production
Hard to find
Buy what you find

Jacob Smithline welcomed his fifth daughter, Adele, into this world on December 3, 1903. The family's tailoring shop provided a comfortable home in New York City, and the girls thrived in the warm, closed surroundings.

Adele learned to appreciate good fabrics and fine needlework under her father's tutelage. She gained practical experience and polished her skills making the wardrobes that her sisters wore proudly to school.

She graduated from Wadleigh High School at the tender age of 16. Her older sister was working at Ben Gershel's in the garment industry, and Adele was quick to follow.

There she earned enough to pay her own way to attend the Pratt Institute where she received a degree in fashion design. In just three years, she earned a promotion to head designer at Gershel's.

From there she went on to the William Bass firm where she was the chief designer. It was reported that Alfred Lasher of Mary Lee Fashions counted it a feather in his cap when she later joined his firm.

Little did Adele dream that the path she had chosen at Mary Lee Fashions would soon be strewn with hearts and flowers. In 1928, she and Wesley William Simpson fell victim to Cupid's arrows. Wesley, a silk salesman, and Adele were married on October 8, 1930, two months short of her twenty-seventh birthday.

Mary Lee Fashions allowed Adele Simpson to put her label on her designs. Her name was soon found as well on an extended line of accessories for the well-dressed woman. Perfume, lingerie, and jewelry all bore her name.

The jewelry was limited in production, so finding it is a rare treat. In 1946, she received the Neiman Marcus Fashion Award and in 1947, the Coty American Fashion Critic Award. Her natural fashion talent was passed on to her son and daugh-

ter. Joan Ellen Raines became her mother's assistant, and her son Jeffrey managed the Simpson perfume line.

Blue bead necklace, bracelet, and earring parure. $550.00.

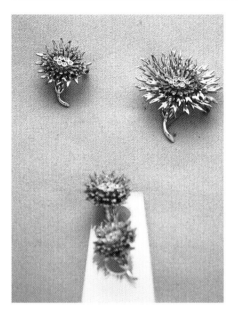

Pavé diamente pansy. $95.00.

Pink rhinestone flower bud with clear rhinestone stamen and green rhinestone leaves. $160.00

Twin chrysanthemum brooches, gold-plated, diamente rhinestone centers. Matching earrings. $375.00.

Sterling brooch, crystals in ajour settings. Faceted 1" center topaz crystal. $295.00.

Faux pearl, blue rhinestone brooch, green rhinestone leaves. $185.00.

2¼" sterling turtle with various shaped dark and light green rhinestones. $125.00.

Fabulous Imitators

Craftsmen emigrating from the old country brought their trades with them. Their years of experience in the European fine jewelry firms artfully equipped them to use precious metals (gold, platinum, and silver), and exquisite gemstones (diamonds, rubies, emeralds, and sapphires).

In the New World, those skills were used to work wonders for the costume jewelry industry. White metal, plating, and rhinestones substituted well for the finer materials as these jewelers worked their miracles.

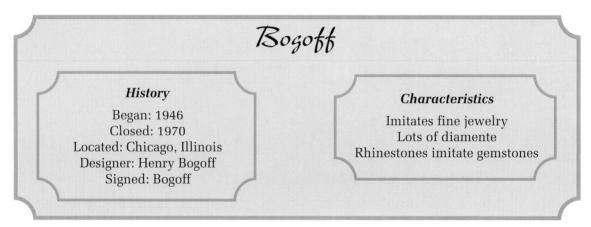

Bogoff

History

Began: 1946
Closed: 1970
Located: Chicago, Illinois
Designer: Henry Bogoff
Signed: Bogoff

Characteristics

Imitates fine jewelry
Lots of diamente
Rhinestones imitate gemstones

The Windy City was home to yet another costume jewelry company, Spear Novelty Company, dating back to the 1920s, specializing in trimmings, buttons, and other accessories. Henry Bogoff was born in Warsaw, Poland, came through Ellis Island in 1908, and settled in New York City where he met the lovely Yvette Glazerman. The young couple moved to Chicago, and Henry found work at the Spear Novelty Company.

Jewels by Bogoff became a reality in 1946. Henry was the designer, Yvette handled the sales and marketing, and Jack Fefferman headed the manufacturing division. Soon the company was supplying Sears & Roebuck, J.C. Penney, Zales, Marshall Fields, and Saks 5th Avenue, eventually reaching third in domestic sales, just behind Coro and Trifari.

So little time, only 24 years, but so much was accomplished. They used precious metal and gemstone techniques to convert designs and rhinestones into jewelry that could be worn in the highest circle of society and yet was affordable for almost everyone.

Most of their designs featured pavé rhinestones and lovely pastel Swarovski quality rhinestones. The clean, sophisticated lines of their designs made Bogoff a timeless fashion that will be enjoyed for generations.

When Henry passed away, Yvette moved back to New York and continued the business, but things weren't the same without Henry's creative drive. Bogoff was among the many jewelry companies that closed their doors in the 1970s.

Limited quantities were produced, so be sure to think twice before passing up this company's jewelry. It belongs in your collector's treasure chest! Truly, jewels from Lake Michigan.

Parure, 1" earrings, each with double links. 7" bracelet has 16 Art Deco links and is 1½" wide. 18" necklace has 33 links. $150.00.

Unusual black bead necklace and earrings. Five strand necklace has black polka dotted beads, silver and black beads, a strand of seed beads, and bugles with eight twisted strands of beads repeated in the last strand. $80.00.

Left: Red baguette earrings with half pavé diamente moon. $55.00. Next: Stretch band bracelet with center row of red rhinestone chatons. $70.00. Top: Diamente rhinestones form chain supporting the draped garland anchored to a red rhinestone ribbon. Each drape is caught by a red chaton. With matching earrings to the right. $195.00.

Silver-plated necklace and earrings sparkle with rhinestones. $145.00.

Diamente loop necklace and earrings. $160.00.

Matching necklace and bracelet feature faux onyx cabochons encircled with clear rhinestones. $130.00.

Left and middle: Matching set of bracelet and necklace has links of blue rhinestones encircled with clear rhinestones. $195.00. Right: Sky blue rhinestones with clear rhinestones. $55.00.

Top: Small clear brooch with two sizes of rhinestones. $38.00. Bottom: Multicolored rhinestone butterfly. $75.00.

Three shades of blue in this group. Left: Necklace has blue and clear rhinestones with a center drop. $80.00. Middle: Blue drop screw-back earrings. $48.00. Right: Ornate blue and clear rhinestone necklace. $95.00.

Left: Small screw-back pavé heart earrings. $30.00. Middle: Clip-on pavé silhouette earrings. $50.00. Right: Hoop earrings move freely inside the overlaid fastener, clip-backs. $95.00.

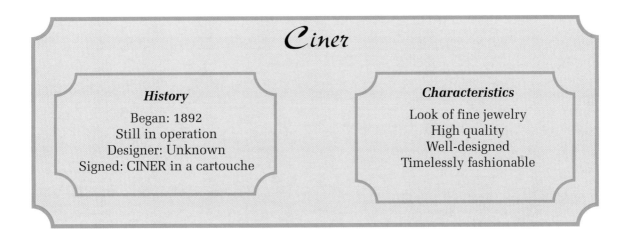

Ciner

History

Began: 1892
Still in operation
Designer: Unknown
Signed: CINER in a cartouche

Characteristics

Look of fine jewelry
High quality
Well-designed
Timelessly fashionable

Emanuel Ciner came to America in 1866, leaving Austria when he was only a year old. By the time he was 27, he had opened his own fine jewelry store in lower Manhattan, offering outstanding wedding and engagement rings.

The story doesn't end there, for the company's history involved four generations of his family as young Ciner began a family legacy that continues today. The only difference between the jewelry made by the fine jeweler Emanuel and his descendants is that today's work is fabulous faux, quality costume jewelry available for a mere fraction of the cost of fine jewelry.

His son Irwin apprenticed at his father's side in 1920 and spent 59 years in the company before handing the reins to his daughter Pat and son-in-law David Hill.

The year 1930 marks when Ciner offered their first costume jewelry line, making history as the only fine jewelry company to convert completely to costume jewelry.

Ciner continued to use only the finest quality materials, Swarovski rhinestones, European glass cabochons, and simulated pearls with a cultura finish, never plastic. Each pearl and every bead was hand strung and hand knotted.

Some call the company the quiet giant because of their contribution of so many fine designs, ones so timeless that Ciner is still using some from the 1940s and 1950s. Ciner has a line of over 7,500 pieces that include pearls, enamels, classic gold, rhinestones, and evening jewels. They proudly use the company logo, "the Tiffany of Costume Jewelry."

Just see for yourself how the following pieces back up their claim.

Emerald and diamond brooch? No, it is emerald-colored rhinestones stems with leaves of pavé diamente. $165.00.

263

Brooch and earrings set. Brooch features green and red glass cabochons. Clear rhinestones enhance the sparkle in both pieces. $95.00.

Left: Gold-plated bracelet with beads of faux turquoise. $70.00. Top: Brooch features clear rhinestones. $65.00.

Left: Five strand pearl bracelet with clear rhinestone clasp and safety chain. $75.00. Right: Clear rhinestone evening bracelet. $125.00.

Flexible, gold-plated necklace. $95.00.

Left: My little pony with rhinestone mane, tail, and saddle. $65.00. Right: Gold-plated burro has a straw hat to protect him from the sun and a rhinestone saddle blanket to ease his burdens. $78.00. Bottom: Square topaz cabochon earrings. $40.00.

Top: White enamel, gold-plated bug. $65.00. Bottom: This gold-plated bug has a faux pearl body. $48.00.

Until we meet again
Sparkles

P. S. The above brooch is a Hattie Carnegie. $150.00

Glossary

Amethyst – natural gemstone in shades from lavender to purple. Costume jewelry frequently uses imitation rhinestones in the same shades.

Antique – costume jewelry made before 1950.

Art Deco – style of geometric lines and bold colors. Period of time, 1910 – 1930.

Art Moderne – 1935 – 1945 art trend combining phenolics and modern metals (e.g., Bakelite and chromium).

Art Nouveau – the designs centered on a poetic interpretation of nature. Period of time, 1890 – 1915.

Articulate – divided into distinct segments that give the piece mobility.

Aurora borealis – microscopic layers of different materials vacuum plated to glass for an iridescent coating.

Baguette – elongated, faceted, straight-sided stones.

Base metal – see white metal.

Bib – a necklace with three or more strands interwoven in a pattern to flow as one.

Black diamond – smoky colored rhinestones. Name given by the Weiss Company.

Brass – alloy of copper, tin, and zinc. Dull yellow metal. Earlier antique costume jewelry piece sometimes used brass as the base metal.

Bridge – suspended arch affixed on each end, decorative.

Brooch – from the French "broche" which means skewer.

Burrs – small lumps of metal rising from the base metal and stationed around the stone to protect them from damage.

Cabochons – unfaceted, rounded, dome stones. Usually flat on underneath side.

Carnival glass – American-made iridescent glassware, imitated in rhinestones.

Cartouche – plate bearing company name, applied to back of jewelry.

Chatelaine – formerly, long chains fastened at the waist that were hung with items necessary daily to a house-keeper. Now it is the name for two brooches connected by one or more chains.

Chaton – most common faceted rhinestone. A cut with 9 to 12 facets, flat table-top surface, bottom comes to a point.

Clip-mate – track brooch frame into which two clips slide. Made by Trifari.

Citrine – quartz stone ranging from yellow to gold in color. Imitated in rhinestones.

Collectibles – costume jewelry manufactured after 1950.

Costume jewelry – jewelry not containing precious jewels or metals.

Crackle glass – lumpy molded glass.

Diamente – imitation diamonds. Another name for clear rhinestones.

Demi-parure – two matching pieces of the same design. Frequently called a set.

Dentelles – unfoiled, crystal glass, formed in a mold and hand cut. Popular from 1930 to 1950s.

Dichroic – having the property of presenting different colors in two different directions, by transmitted light.

Dress clip – hinged clasp brooch worn singularly or in pairs. Inserted on the neckline, bunching the material together to create a lower neckline with ornamentation.

Duette – two clips mounted on a brooch frame. Made by Coro.

Facets – cuts made to shape stones and enhance lights.

Faux – French for "false." Used to denote man-made copies of gem stones.

Filigree – open, airy, lacey, decorative metal wire scroll work.

Flat-back – used to describe a stone that is flat on the back.

Foil backing – backing applied to rhinestones in a vacuum plating process using very thin gold or silver metal. This allows light to bounce off the stone and sparkle.

Fur clip – a decorative clip with two long prongs on a spring steel to be worn on a heavy fabric or fur.

Hallmark – mark on back of jewelry denoting gold or silver content.

Hang tag – removable paper or metal tag bearing company name, attached after production is completed.

Japanned – finishing processing using a black, coal-tar derivative.

Key stones – long slender stones, narrower at one end, made especially for the Schreiner Company.

Lucite – acrylic plastic, transparent. DuPont trade name for Plexiglas.

Marquise – see navette.

Navette – stone, oval-shaped with point on each end, resembling an eye. Also called marquise.

Nodder – individual pieces mounted on small springs to vibrate when moved. Also called a trembler.

Opalene – man-made imitation of opal.

Parure – more than two matching pieces of jewelry.

Pavé – stones placed so close together with a minimum of metal showing. Literally "paving over the metal."

Phrygian cap – symbol of the French military head gear, used by Marcel Boucher.

Pillbox – small container carried in purse to hold medications.

Plating – process of dipping jewelry in copper, then in electro-magnetic acid bath which forms a thin layer of finish.

Pot metal – see white metal.

Rhinestone – leaded glass stones with foil backing.

Rhodium – non-tarnishing silver-colored finish. Member of the platinum group of metals.

Scatter pins – a group of common theme small pins, usually two or three in a set.

Set – more than one matching piece of the same design.

Suite – more than two pieces of the same design, also called a parure.

Sweater guards – two alligator pinch clips chained together. Used to hold cardigan sweater front together.

Topaz – gemstone usually ranging in color from yellow to orange.

Trademark – name of company placed on back of jewelry.

Vacuum plated – name of process used to foil the backs of rhinestones.

Vermeil – a gold wash over sterling silver. Can be pink or yellow gold finish.

White metal – 92% tin with added cadmium, lead, and zinc. Used to form the first stage of costume jewelry. Also called base or pot metal.

Bibliography

Baker, Lillian, *50 Years of Collectible Fashion Jewelry, 1925 -– 1975,* Collector Books, Paducah, Ky., 1995.

Ball, Joanne Dubbs/Torem, Dorothy Hehl, *Costume Jewelers, Golden Age of Design,* Schiffer Publishing, Ltd., Atglen, Pa., 1990.

Becker, Vivienne, *Fabulous Costume Jewelry,* Schiffer Publishing Ltd., Atglen, Pa., 1993.

Brown, Marcia Sparkles, *Hidden Treasures,* (seven videos), Venture Entertainment Studio, Los Angeles, Calif., 1998 – 2001.

Brown, Marcia Sparkles, *Unsigned Beauties of Costume Jewelry,* Collector Books, Paducah, Ky., 2000.

Brynialti, Carla/Roberto, *American Costume Jewelry*, Gabriele Mazzotta, Milan, Italy, 1997.

Cera, Deanna Farretti, *The Jewels of Miriam Haskell,* Ideal, Milan, Italy, 1997.

Cera, Deanna Faretti, *Jewels of Fantasy*, Abrams, New York, N.Y., 1992.

Cera, Deanna Farretti, *Amazing Gems*, Harry N. Abrams, Inc., New York, N.Y., 1997.

Dolan, Maryanne, *Collecting Rhinestone & Colored Jewelry,* Books Americana, Florence, Ala., 1990.

Ettinger, Roseann, *Popular Jewelry, 1840 – 1940,* Schiffer Publishing Ltd., Atglen, Pa., 1990.

Ettinger, Roseann, *Popular Jewelry 40's & 50's,* Schiffer Publishing Ltd., Atglen, Pa., 1994.

Ettinger, Roseann, *Popular Jewelry of the 60's, 70's & 80's,* Schiffer Publishing Ltd., Atglen, Pa., 1997.

Gallina, Jill, *Christmas Pins, Past & Present,* Schiffer Publishing Ltd., Atglen, Pa., 1996.

Gordon, Angie, *Twentieth Century Costume Jewelry,* Adasia International, Carle Place, N.Y., 1990.

Kovel's, *Identifying 20th Century Costume & Silver Jewelry, Antiques, Inc.,* Pepper Pike, Ohio, 1995.

Lane, Kenneth Jay/Miller, Harrice Simmons, *Faking It,* Harry N. Abrams, Inc., New York, N.Y., 1996.

Miller, Harrice Simmons, *Costume Jewelry – Confident Collector, Avon,* New York, N.Y., 1994.

Newman, Harold, *An Illustrated Dictionary of Jewelry,* Thames & Hudston, Inc., New York, N.Y., 1981.

Rainwater, Dorothy, *American Jewelry Manufacturers,* Schiffer Publishing, Ltd., Atglen, Pa., 1988.

Rezazadeh, Fred, *Costume Jewelry,* Collector Books, Paducah, Ky., 1998.

Romero, Christie, *Hidden Treasures,* (video), Venture Entertainment Studios, Los Angeles, Calif., 1999.

Romero, Christie, *Warman's Jewelry*, Krause, Iola, Wisc., 1998.

Schiffer, Nancy, *The Best of Costume Jewelry,* Schiffer Publishing Ltd., Atglen, Pa., 1996.

Schiffer, Nancy, *Costume Jewelry – The Great Pretenders,* Schiffer Publishing Ltd., Atglen, Pa., 1996.

Schiffer, Nancy, *Rhinestones,* Schiffer Publishing Ltd., Atglen, Pa., 1993.

Shatz, Sheryl Gross, *What's It Made Of,* Benjamin Shatz, Santa Ana, Calif., 1992.

Simonds, Cheri, *Collectible Costume Jewelry,* Collector Books, Paducah, Ky., 1997.

Tolkein, Tracy/Wilkinson, Henrietta, *A Collector's Guide to Costume Jewelry,* Firefly Books, Ltd., Willowdale Conn., 1997.

Index

COLLECTOR BOOKS
Informing Today's Collector

DOLLS, FIGURES & TEDDY BEARS

2079	**Barbie** Doll Fashion, Volume I, Eames	$24.95
3957	**Barbie** Exclusives, Rana	$18.95
5672	The **Barbie** Doll Years, 4th Edition, Olds	$19.95
3810	**Chatty Cathy** Dolls, Lewis	$15.95
4559	Collectible **Action Figures**, 2nd Ed., Manos	$17.95
2211	Collector's Ency. of **Madame Alexander Dolls**, 1965 – 1990, Smith	$24.95
4863	Collector's Encyclopedia of **Vogue Dolls**, Stover/Izen	$29.95
1799	**Effanbee Dolls**, Smith	$19.95
5611	**Madame Alexander** Store Exclusives & Limited Editions, Crowsey	$24.95
5689	**Nippon Dolls** & Playthings, Van Patten/Lau	$29.95
5253	Story of **Barbie**, 2nd Ed., Westenhouser	$24.95
1513	**Teddy Bears & Steiff** Animals, Mandel	$9.95
1817	**Teddy Bears & Steiff** Animals, 2nd Series, Mandel	$19.95
2084	**Teddy Bears, Annalee's & Steiff** Animals, 3rd Series, Mandel	$19.95
1808	Wonder of **Barbie**, Manos	$9.95
1430	World of **Barbie** Dolls, Manos	$9.95
4880	World of **Raggedy Ann** Collectibles, Avery	$24.95

TOYS, MARBLES & CHRISTMAS COLLECTIBLES

2333	Antique & Collectible **Marbles**, 3rd Ed., Grist	$9.95
5353	**Breyer Animal** Collector's Guide, I.D. and Values, 2nd ed., Browell	$19.95
4976	**Christmas Ornaments**, Lights & Decorations, Johnson	$24.95
4737	**Christmas Ornaments**, Lights & Decorations, Vol. II, Johnson	$24.95
4739	**Christmas Ornaments**, Lights & Decorations, Vol. III, Johnson	$24.95
2338	Collector's Encyclopedia of **Disneyana**, Longest, Stern	$24.95
5038	Collector's Guide to **Diecast Toys** & Scale Models, 2nd Ed., Johnson	$19.95
5681	Collector's Guide to **Lunchboxes**, White	$19.95
4566	Collector's Guide to **Tootsietoys**, 2nd Ed, Richter	$19.95
5360	**Fisher-Price Toys**, Cassity	$19.95
4945	**G-Men and FBI Toys**, Whitworth	$18.95
5593	Grist's Big Book of **Marbles**, 2nd Ed.	$24.95
3970	Grist's Machine-Made & Contemporary **Marbles**, 2nd Ed.	$9.95
5267	**Matchbox Toys**, 3rd Ed., 1947 to 1998, Johnson	$19.95
5830	**McDonald's** Collectibles, Henriques/DuVall	$24.95
5673	Modern **Candy Containers** & Novelties, Brush/Miller	$19.95
1540	Modern **Toys** 1930–1980, Baker	$19.95
3888	**Motorcycle Toys**, Antique & Contemporary, Gentry/Downs	$18.95
5693	Schroeder's Collectible **Toys**, Antique to Modern Price Guide, 7th Ed	$17.95

JEWELRY, HATPINS, WATCHES & PURSES

1712	Antique & Collectible **Thimbles** & Accessories, Mathis	$19.95
1748	Antique **Purses**, Revised Second Ed., Holiner	$19.95
1278	Art Nouveau & Art Deco **Jewelry**, Baker	$9.95
4850	Collectible **Costume Jewelry**, Simonds	$24.95
5675	Collectible **Silver Jewelry**, Rezazadeh	$24.95
3722	Collector's Ency. of **Compacts**, Carryalls & Face Powder Boxes, Mueller	$24.95
4940	**Costume Jewelry**, A Practical Handbook & Value Guide, Rezazadeh	$24.95
1716	Fifty Years of Collectible Fashion **Jewelry**, 1925-1975, Baker	$19.95
1424	**Hatpins** & Hatpin Holders, Baker	$9.95
5695	**Ladies' Vintage Accessories**, Bruton	$24.95
1181	100 Years of Collectible **Jewelry**, 1850 – 1950, Baker	$9.95
5696	Vintage & Vogue Ladies' **Compacts**, 2nd Edition, Gerson	$29.95

FURNITURE

1457	American **Oak** Furniture, McNerney	$9.95
3716	American **Oak** Furniture, Book II, McNerney	$12.95
1118	Antique **Oak** Furniture, Hill	$7.95
2132	Collector's Encyclopedia of **American** Furniture, Vol. I, Swedberg	$24.95
2271	Collector's Encyclopedia of **American** Furniture, Vol. II, Swedberg	$24.95
3720	Collector's Encyclopedia of **American** Furniture, Vol. III, Swedberg	$24.95
5359	Early **American** Furniture, Obbard	$12.95
1755	Furniture of the **Depression Era**, Swedberg	$19.95
3906	**Heywood-Wakefield** Modern Furniture, Rouland	$18.95
1885	**Victorian** Furniture, Our American Heritage, McNerney	$9.95
3829	**Victorian** Furniture, Our American Heritage, Book II, McNerney	$9.95

INDIANS, GUNS, KNIVES, TOOLS, PRIMITIVES

1868	Antique **Tools**, Our American Heritage, McNerney	$9.95
1426	**Arrowheads** & Projectile Points, Hothem	$7.95
5616	Big Book of **Pocket Knives**, Stewart	$19.95
2279	**Indian Artifacts** of the Midwest, Hothem	$14.95
5685	**Indian Artifacts** of the Midwest, Book IV, Hothem	$19.95
5687	Modern **Guns**, Identification & Values, 13th Ed., Quertermous	$14.95

2164	**Primitives**, Our American Heritage, McNerney	$9.95
1759	**Primitives**, Our American Heritage, Series II, McNerney	$14.95
4730	Standard **Knife** Collector's Guide, 3rd Ed., Ritchie & Stewart	$12.95

PAPER COLLECTIBLES & BOOKS

4633	**Big Little Books**, A Collector's Reference & Value Guide, Jacobs	$18.95
4710	Collector's Guide to **Children's Books**, 1850 to 1950, Jones	$18.95
5596	Collector's Guide to **Children's Books**, 1950 to 1975, Jones	$19.95
1441	Collector's Guide to **Post Cards**, Wood	$9.95
2081	Guide to Collecting **Cookbooks**, Allen	$14.95
2080	Price Guide to **Cookbooks** & Recipe Leaflets, Dickinson	$9.95
3973	**Sheet Music** Reference & Price Guide, 2nd Ed., Pafik & Guiheen	$19.95
4654	**Victorian Trade Cards**, Historical Reference & Value Guide, Cheadle	$19.95
4733	**Whitman Juvenile Books**, Brown	$17.95

OTHER COLLECTIBLES

2269	Antique **Brass & Copper** Collectibles, Gaston	$16.95
1880	Antique **Iron**, McNerney	$9.95
3872	Antique **Tins**, Dodge	$24.95
5607	Antiquing and Collecting on the **Internet**, Parry	$12.95
1128	**Bottle** Pricing Guide, 3rd Ed., Cleveland	$7.95
3718	Collectible **Aluminum**, Grist	$16.95
4560	Collectible **Cats**, An Identification & Value Guide, Book II, Fyke	$19.95
5676	Collectible **Souvenir Spoons**, Book II, Bednersh	$29.95
5666	Collector's Encyclopedia of **Granite Ware**, Book II, Greguire	$29.95
4857	Collector's Guide to **Art Deco**, 2nd Ed., Gaston	$17.95
5608	Collector's Guide to Buying, Selling, & Trading on the **Internet**, 2nd Ed., Hix	$12.95
4887	Collector's Guide to **Creek Chub Lures** & Collectibles, Smith	$24.95
3966	Collector's Guide to **Inkwells**, Identification & Values, Badders	$18.95
3881	Collector's Guide to **Novelty Radios**, Bunis/Breed	$18.95
5621	Collector's Guide to **Online Auctions**, Hix	$12.95
4652	Collector's Guide to **Transistor Radios**, 2nd Ed., Bunis	$16.95
4864	Collector's Guide to **Wallace Nutting Pictures**, Ivankovich	$18.95
1629	**Doorstops**, Identification & Values, Bertoia	$9.95
5683	**Fishing Lure Collectibles**, 2nd Ed., Murphy/Edmisten	$29.95
5259	**Flea Market Trader**, 12th Ed., Huxford	$9.95
3819	**General Store** Collectibles, Wilson	$24.95
2216	**Kitchen Antiques**, 1790–1940, McNerney	$14.95
5686	**Lighting Fixtures** of the Depression Era, Book I, Thomas	$24.95
4950	The **Lone Ranger**, Collector's Reference & Value Guide, Felbinger	$18.95
5603	19th Century **Fishing Lures**, Carter	$29.95
2026	**Railroad** Collectibles, 4th Ed., Baker	$14.95
5619	**Roy Rogers and Dale Evans** Toys & Memorabilia, Coyle	$24.95
1632	**Salt & Pepper Shakers**, Guarnaccia	$9.95
5091	**Salt & Pepper Shakers** II, Guarnaccia	$18.95
3443	**Salt & Pepper Shakers** IV, Guarnaccia	$18.95
5007	**Silverplated Flatware**, Revised 4th Edition, Hagan	$18.95
3892	**Toy & Miniature Sewing Machines**, Thomas	$18.95
5144	Value Guide to **Advertising Memorabilia**, 2nd Ed., Summers	$19.95
3977	Value Guide to **Gas Station Memorabilia**, Summers	$24.95
4877	Vintage **Bar Ware**, Visakay	$24.95
4935	The W.F. Cody **Buffalo Bill** Collector's Guide with Values, Wojtowicz	$24.95
5281	**Wanted to Buy**, 7th Edition	$9.95

GLASSWARE & POTTERY

4929	**American Art Pottery**, 1880 – 1950, Sigafoose	$24.95
5358	Collector's Encyclopedia of **Depression Glass**, 14th Ed., Florence	$19.95
5748	Collector's Encyclopedia of **Fiesta**, 9th Ed., Huxford	$19.95
4946	Collector's Encyclopedia of **Howard Pierce Porcelain**, Dommel	$24.95
5609	Collector's Encyclopedia of **Limoges Porcelain**, 3rd Ed., Gaston	$29.95
1358	Collector's Encyclopedia of **McCoy Pottery**, Huxford	$19.95
5677	Collector's Encyclopedia of **Niloak**, 2nd Edition, Gifford	$29.95
5678	Collector's Encyclopedia of **Nippon Porcelain**, 6th Series, Van Patten	$29.95
5618	Collector's Encyclopedia of **Rosemeade Pottery**, Dommel	$24.95
5680	Collector's Guide to **Feather Edge Ware**, McAllister	$19.95
2339	Collector's Guide to **Shawnee Pottery**, Vanderbilt	$19.95
1523	Colors in **Cambridge Glass**, National Cambridge Society	$19.95
4714	**Czechoslovakian Glass** and Collectibles, Book II, Barta	$16.95
5528	Early American **Pattern Glass**, Metz	$17.95
5257	**Fenton Art Glass** Patterns, 1939 – 1980, Whitmyer	$29.95
5261	**Fostoria Tableware**, 1924 – 1943, Long/Seate	$24.95
5691	**Post86 Fiesta**, Identification & Value Guide, Racheter	$19.95
5617	Standard Encyclopedia of **Pressed Glass**, 2nd Ed., Edwards/Carwile	$29.95

This is only a partial listing of the books on collectibles that are available from Collector Books. All books are well illustrated and contain current values. Most of our books are available from your local bookseller, antique dealer, or public library. If you are unable to locate certain titles in your area, you may order by mail from COLLECTOR BOOKS, P.O. Box 3009, Paducah, KY 42002-3009. Customers with Visa, MasterCard, or Discover may phone in orders from 7:00–5:00 CST, Monday–Friday, Toll Free 1-800-626-5420, or online at www.collectorbooks.com. Add $3.00 for postage for the first book ordered and 50¢ for each additional book. Include item number, title, and price when ordering. Allow 14 to 21 days for delivery.

Schroeder's ANTIQUES Price Guide

OUR #1 BEST-SELLER!

...is the #1 bestselling antiques & collectibles value guide on the market today, and here's why...

• *More than 450 advisors, well-known dealers, and top-notch collectors work together with our editors to bring you accurate information regarding pricing and identification.*

• *More than 50,000 items in over 600 categories are listed along with hundreds of sharp original photos that illustrate not only the rare and unusual, but the common, popular collectibles as well.*

• *Each large close-up shot shows important details clearly. Every subject is represented with histories and background information, a feature not found in any of our competitors' publications.*

• *Our editors keep abreast of newly developing trends, often adding several new categories a year as the need arises.*

8½" x 11"
608 pages
$14.95

If it merits the interest of today's collector, you'll find it in *Schroeder's*. And you can feel confident that the information we publish is up-to-date and accurate. Our advisors thoroughly check each category to spot inconsistencies, listings that may not be entirely reflective of market dealings, and lines too vague to be of merit. Only the best of the lot remains for publication.

Without doubt, you'll find
Schroeder's Antiques Price Guide
the only one to buy for reliable information and values.

cb

COLLECTOR BOOKS
P.O. Box 3009 • Paducah, KY 42002–3009
www.collectorbooks.com